Xunzi

TRANSLATIONS FROM THE ASIAN CLASSICS

Translations from the Asian Classics

Xunzi BASIC WRITINGS

Translated by
BURTON WATSON

Columbia University Press *New York*

Columbia University Press
Publishers Since 1893
New York
Chichester, West Sussex

Copyright © 2003 Columbia University Press
All rights reserved

Library of Congress Cataloging-in-Publication Data
Xunzi, 340–245 B.C.
[Xunzi. English Selections]
p. cm. — (Translations from the Asian classics)
Includes index.
ISBN 978-0-231-12965-7 (pbk.)
I. Watson, Burton, 1925– II. Title. III. Series.
B128.H68 E5 2003
181'.112—dc21   2002035168

Contents

OUTLINE OF EARLY CHINESE HISTORY

(Dates and entries before 841 B.C. are traditional)

B.C.	Dynasty		
2852		Culture Heroes	Fu Xi, inventor of writing, fishing, trapping.
2737			Shen Nong, inventor of agriculture, commerce.
2697			Yellow Emperor.
2357		Sage Kings	Yao.
2255			Shun.
2205	Xia Dynasty		Yu, virtuous founder of dynasty.
1818			Jie, degenerate terminator of dynasty.
1766	Shang or Yin Dynasty		King Tang, virtuous founder of dynasty.
[c. 1300]			[Beginning of archeological evidence.]
1154			Zhou, degenerate terminator of dynasty.

Date	Dynasty	Event
	Three Dynasties	
1122		King Wen, virtuous founder of dynasty.
1115	Zhou Dynasty — Western Zhou	King Wu, virtuous founder of dynasty.
		King Cheng, virtuous founder of dynasty.
		(Duke of Zhou, regent to King Cheng)
878		King Li.
781		King You.
771		
722	Eastern Zhou	Spring and Autumn period (722–481).
551		Period of the "hundred philosophers" (551–c. 233): Confucius, Mozi, Laozi (?), Mencius, Zhuangzi, Hui Shi, Shang Yang, Gongsun Long, Xunzi, Han Feizi.
403		Warring States period (403–221).
4th to 3rd cent.		Extensive wall-building and waterworks by Qin and other states.
249	Qin Dynasty (221–207 B.C.)	Lu Buwei, prime minister of Qin.
221		The First Emperor; Li Si, prime minister.
214		The Great Wall completed.

Preface

Where does human goodness—insofar as there is such a commodity—come from? Is it inborn in the individual, only waiting to shine forth when the occasion presents itself? Or is it something artificially instilled from outside, the product of rigorous training and discipline?

Among Chinese philosophers, Xunzi is perhaps remembered primarily for the latter view, dourly asserting that human nature is basically evil. His fellow countrymen, who despite severe buffeting at the hands of history have over the centuries maintained a surprisingly optimistic outlook on life, have never really gone along with him in this. They prefer instead the opinion of his eminent predecessor, Mencius, that people are intrinsically good, or Buddhist assurances that all living beings have latent within them the "seeds" or potential for moral and spiritual perfection.

In Xunzi's philosophical system as a whole, his bleak assessment of human nature is probably of less interest today than are the highly sanguine hopes he holds out for the improvement of that nature through education and moral training, and particularly through the civilizing influence of rites and music. And, it should be noted, like many other Chinese thinkers, he believes that the rulers of the nation—government, in other words—should play a crucial role in this process of educating and uplifting the population.

Our own society is very much alive with debate over how big or how little government ought to be, what its role should be in the lives of citizens, what the aim and content of education should be and through what channels it is best administered. The particular terms in which Xunzi's arguments are presented may in some cases seem odd or irrelevant to readers today. But many of the questions he addresses—how to ensure the sane use of language, to deploy military power effectively, to bring about order and safety in society—and those pertaining to education and the role of government mentioned earlier are surprisingly close to the concerns of our own age. Though the solutions he proposes may not strike us as entirely feasible, we can still learn much by observing the process of reasoning and analysis that leads to them. I am gratified that this translation of the more important of Xunzi's writings continues to be made available to readers.

Xunzi

⤐ INTRODUCTION

What little is known of the life of Xunzi, or Master Xun, is culled from evidence in his own writings and from the brief biography of him written by the historian Sima Qian some hundred years or so after his death, which forms part of Chapter 74 of the *Shiji*. His personal name was Kuang,[1] and he was a native of Zhao, a state situated in the central part of northern China. The date of his birth is unknown, but it was probably around 312 B.C., when his famous predecessor in the Confucian school, Mencius, was already well along in years. Nothing whatever is known of his early life; we hear of him first at the age of fifty, journeying to the court of the state of Qi to study and teach.

In 386 B.C. the Tians, who for generations had served as ministers to the royal family of Qi, usurped the throne of Qi and set themselves up as its new rulers. In order to consolidate

---

[1]He is often referred to as Xun Qing or Qingzi, though it is not certain whether Qing is a name or an honorary title like "lord." His surname is frequently written with the character for "grandson," pronounced Sun in modern Chinese; perhaps the two characters Xun and Sun were homophones in ancient Chinese, though other explanations are offered.

their power and prove their fitness for so lofty a station, these new rulers of the Tian family, particularly the second major one, King Xuan (reigned 342–324 B.C.), encouraged scholars from other regions to come to the court of Qi by offering them honorary titles, stipends, living quarters, and complete leisure to pursue their studies and expound their various doctrines. Before long Qi had become the leading center of intellectual activity in China; Mencius visited the state during the reign of King Xuan and many other well known philosophers resided there permanently.

By the time Xunzi arrived in Qi, probably around 264 B.C., the ranks of government-supported scholars attracted by King Xuan and his successors had been thinned by death, and Xunzi was welcomed as an eminent elder and honored with titles and marks of esteem. Because of slanderous talk against him, however, he eventually left Qi and went south to the state of Chu, where the lord of Chunshen, nominally the prime minister of Chu but virtually its ruler, appointed him to the post of magistrate of Lanling, a region in southern Shandong. The Lord of Chunshen was assassinated by a court rival in 238 B.C. (the only date in Xunzi's life that can be fixed with certainty), and Xunzi lost his post as magistrate, but remained in Lanling the rest of his life and was buried there. The date of his death is unknown, so it is impossible to say whether he lived to witness the final unification of China under the First Emperor of the Qin, which was completed in 221 B.C.

The book which bears his name indicates that Xunzi visited the state of Qin, probably during the period 266–255 B.C., and that he debated military affairs in the presence of King Xiaocheng (reigned 265–245 B.C.) of his native state of Zhao. He undoubtedly had many disciples, and it is unfortunate for his reputation as a Confucian that the two most famous of them should have been Han Feizi, who became the leading exponent of the Legalist school, and Li Si, the statesman who assisted the First Emperor of the Qin in the unification of the empire, both men whose names are inseparably linked with the ridicule and persecution of Confucianism.

Xunzi's life, then, or what can be known of it, was a long and rather quiet one of teaching and study, with a minor excursion into local political administration. Later scholars have marveled that his worth, like that of Confucius and Mencius, should have been so little recognized by the political leaders of his time, and that he should have been allowed to live and die in relative obscurity. But the rulers of China, it seems, were not yet ready to give serious ear to the teachings of the Confucian school.

In Xunzi's day China was dominated by three powerful states: Qi in the east, Chu in the south, and Qin in the west. In the northwest and northeast four or five smaller states, among them Xunzi's native state of Zhao, maintained a precarious existence by allying themselves with one or another of the major powers. The old ruling house of Zhou, which once claimed sovereignty over all these so-called feudal states, had dwindled into utter insignificance, its territory shrunken to a tiny area in the center of China, its ancient ritual vessels and emblems of authority eyed with greed by its neighbors, and in 249 B.C. the dynasty finally passed out of existence altogether. For the first time in history, if traditional accounts are to be believed, China was left without even a nominal Son of Heaven, and no one knew where to turn his eyes in the hope of peace and unity. Known as the era of the Warring States, this period was an age of political instability and ferment, of incessant intrigue and strife.

Paradoxically, it was also an age of prosperity and cultural progress. Trade flourished, cities increased in size, men traveled freely from one state to another, and literacy and learning spread beyond the narrow confines of the ruling class. Even the art of warfare, though a melancholy index of progress, achieved a scale and complexity undreamed of in earlier days.

The rulers of the various states, roused by the fierce competition for survival, cast about for ways to improve the efficiency of their administration, win the support of their people, and enrich their domains. In response to their call, thinker after thinker came forward to offer his analysis of the problem and propound his solution. Return to the ways of antiquity, make better use of the land, lessen your desires, love the people, leave things alone!—advice swamped the rulers, and each set about assiduously applying that which took his fancy.

Xunzi lived at the very end of this period, and therefore in his solution to the ills of the time he was able to draw upon the speculations and suggestions of his predecessors, at the same time refuting what he believed to be their errors. His thought is thus marked by eclecticism, embracing a strain of Daoist quietism, a hard-headed realism reminiscent of the Legalist writers, a concern for the correct use of terminology which he had learned from the philosophers of the school of Logic, and other borrowings which, if more of the writings of his predecessors were extant, could undoubtedly be identified with greater certainty.

Again, perhaps because of the advantage he enjoyed in being able to survey the entire range of ancient thought, Xunzi's work represents the most complete and well-ordered philosophical system of the early period. It is so well ordered and integrated, in fact, that one scarcely knows where to begin in describing it, since each part fits into and locks with all the others. The core of it is the ethical and political teachings of Confucius and his disciples, but around this core cluster areas of investigation and speculation that were hardly touched upon in earlier Confucian writing.

As a philosophical system, Xunzi's thought rests upon the harsh initial thesis that man's nature is basically evil. Considering the cutthroat age he lived in, this is not a surprising conclusion, and it allows him to place tremendous emphasis upon the need for education and moral training. But it flatly contradicts the view of Mencius, who taught that man is naturally inclined to goodness, and in later centuries, when Mencius's view came to be regarded as the orthodox one, it led to an unhappy clouding of Xunzi's entire system of thought.

To this dark initial thesis Xunzi contraposes the almost unlimitedly bright possibilities for improvement through study and moral training. The subject of this study is to be the classical texts, the rituals and ritual principles created for man's guidance by the sages of the past and present; and the teachers are to be the sages themselves. Are we to assume, then, that these sages, the saviors of mankind from inborn evil, belong to some species apart? Absolutely not, replies Xunzi. The sages in their basic nature and desires are exactly like all other men; only, as he explains in a strikingly modern chapter on epistemology and psychology, they have learned to employ their minds in such a way as to attain moral understanding and insight. And on the basis of this understanding they are able to define correctly the ethical relationships that govern the hierarchical order of society, the order which distinguishes man from the beasts.

The proper end of this process of education, the proper function of the sage, is to govern. Once he has become not only sage and teacher, but ruler as well, he may, as Xunzi explains in his chapters on political science, economics and ritual, set about ordering the state on the basis of proper moral principles and insuring peace and prosperity to the world. Like so many of his predecessors and contemporaries, Xunzi frequently harks back to the golden ages of the past—the reigns of the sage rulers Yao,

Shun, Yu, King Tang of the Shang dynasty, and Kings Wen and Wu of the Zhou—as examples of such periods of ideal peace and order. But, unlike most Confucian philosophers, he also urges men to observe the examples of later rulers of virtue, who lived in the less distant past and whose ways are therefore easier to learn about and to practice. Xunzi maintained that, although political and social conditions invariably change, human nature and basic moral principles do not, and therefore the principles that were correct and brought order in the past will, if faithfully followed, do so again. He is thus calling not for a return to the precise ways of antiquity, but for a reconstruction of the moral greatness of antiquity in terms of the present. As he states in one of the sections not translated here, if you apply these eternally valid moral principles of the sages today, "then Shun and Yu will appear again, and the reign of a true king will arise once more" (sec. II).

Xunzi's view of the ideal ruler and his administration is very close to that of Mencius, though Xunzi had less patience than Mencius with the feudal system and declared that hereditary titles[2] should be abolished and men promoted and demoted in the social hierarchy solely on the basis of merit. And, unlike Mencius, he was willing to compromise with the frailty of his age to the extent of describing other easier and less ambitious ways of ruling than simply that of the ideal king, the ruler of perfect virtue. He thus devotes considerable space to discussions of how to become a successful *ba*—dictator or overlord—a ruler who possesses neither the virtue nor the popular sanction of a true king, but who is nevertheless able to insure well-being and stability, if not moral guidance, to his subjects. He himself had vis-

---

[2]Not to be confused with hereditary rights to government offices, which were condemned by Mencius and all late Zhou philosophers alike.

ited the state of Qin, and he had a healthy respect for the military and economic accomplishments of its rulers, though he deplored the harsh and terroristic methods by which such gains had been won. And he was no doubt conscious that Mencius had failed to win acceptance for his ideas from the rulers of the time precisely because he refused to discuss anything but the most uncompromisingly high ideals of political morality.

Finally, like Confucius and Mencius before him, he took care to emphasize that the legitimacy and survival of the ruler rest ultimately upon the support of his people: he is a boat, they the water which may bear him up or capsize him as they choose. No claims of hereditary right or iron discipline can hold out forever in the face of popular indifference or anger; no ruling house can long survive when it has ceased to fulfill the functions for which it was called to office. This was a lesson which Mencius and Xunzi found abundantly clear in the troubled history of their own age, and they were determined to impress it upon the minds of the rulers, to waken them to the full moral responsibilities of government. For they believed that, if the rulers did not wake to and accept these responsibilities, the day would come when the people would rise up, as the peasants of the French Revolution were to do, to ask of their leaders, in the words of Carlyle: "How have ye treated us, how have ye taught us, fed us, and led us, while we toiled for you?"

These, then, are the positive aspects of Xunzi's philosophy, the methods and aims which he would have men adopt. But much of his writing is also concerned with the things he wishes them to reject. First of all he would have them reject all beliefs and practices that seek to put man in contact with the supernatural or to endow him with supernatural powers. Since the mind of man itself is the source of all moral order, and hence of human perfection, such attempts to venture beyond the human realm are to Xunzi pointless and futile. Certain religious or magical practices he condemns outright, such as prayers for rain or for the cure of sickness, or physiognomy, the art of divining a man's future by the configuration of his face. Others he is willing to countenance, such as the art of divination by the tortoise shell and milfoil stalks, or, as in the case of the mourning and sacrificial rites, even willing to encourage, providing that they are interpreted, at least by men of intellect, in a purely humanistic fashion. In other words, such rites and practices should not be regarded as acts possessing any supernatural efficacy, but as purely human inventions designed to ornament the social life of man and guide him in the proper expression of his emotions. He specifically denies the existence of baleful ghosts or demons (the bugbears with which Mozi hoped to terrify men into good behavior); and though he occasionally used the word *shen*, which in other writers denotes the spirits of the ancestors and of the powers of nature, he defines it as "that which is completely good and fully ordered" (sec. 8), making it a quality of moral excellence. He is thus the most thoroughly rationalistic of the early Confucian writers, and since sections of his work, particularly those dealing with mourning and sacrificial rites, were incorporated in the *Liji* or *Book of Rites*, which became one of the five Confucian Classics, his rationalism has had a very great influence upon later Chinese thought.

He also called upon men to renounce all paths of inquiry that would lead them away from human moral concerns and into (in his opinion) a barren and unending search for knowledge in the realms outside the world of man. Too many of the thinkers of his time, he felt, were directing men into just such paths, or into others equally erroneous, and for this reason he frequently recorded his objections to the various philosophical schools of late Zhou times, often with considerable asperity. (Fairness and restraint in appraising each other's opinions is not a characteristic of early Chinese philosophers, and Xunzi is certainly no exception.)

The chief target of his attacks is Mozi, whose doctrines were for many reasons repugnant to him. He devotes a whole essay to answering Mozi's objections to music, and elsewhere he attacks the Mohist teachings on frugality, social uniformity, and meager burial rites. He criticizes Zhuangzi for dwelling too much on the mystical workings of nature and slighting human concerns, the Legalists for their belief that precise laws can replace the personal leadership of a virtuous ruler, and two other little-known philosophers, Shen Dao and Song Jian, for their doctrines of passivity and the elimination of desire. And in an essay on the correct use of terminology, he replies to the teachings of the logicians Hui Shi and Gongsun Long, whose famous paradoxes and conundrums he felt were endangering the sane and efficient use of language.

Finally, he did not hesitate to condemn what he believed were errors in the doctrines of the Confucian school as well. I have already noted how his theory of human nature directly contradicts that of Mencius, whom he criticizes by name. In another essay (sec. 18), in which he discusses a number of popular misconceptions, he vehemently refutes the legend that the ancient sage ruler Yao selected Shun from among the common people to be his successor and ceded the throne to him. This legend is recorded in the *Book of Documents*, the *Analects*, and the *Mencius*, and was evidently widely accepted among the followers of the Confucian school. Scholars now believe that it is an invention of fairly late Zhou times, and that the passages referring to it in the *Book of Documents* ("Canon of Yao") and the *Analects* (ch. 20) are likewise of late date. Possibly it originated with the followers of the Mohist school, which may explain why Xunzi rejects it so violently (though Mencius accepted it without question). In any event, he is unique among early Confucian writers in doing so, and his objections were completely ignored by later scholars, who unanimously accepted the legend as historical fact.[3]

Xunzi's work therefore represents a critique and appraisal of late Zhou thought as a whole, at the same time presenting the fullest and most systematic exposition of the doctrines of the Confucian school as he understood them. He wrote at a time when the unification of China under a central government was almost in sight, though how clearly he realized this we cannot say. His program for the rule of a unified nation was rejected by the Qin dynasty, which preferred Legalist doctrines, and was temporarily eclipsed by the First Emperor's systematic suppression of Confucianism. But the expeditious fall of the Qin in 207 B.C. discredited the harsh policies of Legalism, and the Confucians once more came forward in an effort to gain a hearing from the leaders of the newly founded Han. Mohism, for reasons not entirely clear, had faded into the background, and Daoism, though favored by several of the prominent statesmen of the time, proved too nebulous and apolitical to serve as the philosophy of a great nation. Han Confucianism, based upon Xunzi's thought but with numerous extraneous elements borrowed from other doctrines, eventually won the day, and toward the end of the second century B.C. was declared the official creed of the Han state.

True, the Han ignored many of Xunzi's most admirable dicta. It granted hereditary titles, a practice he had condemned;

---

[3]It is interesting to note that in 316 B.C. the king of the state of Yan was persuaded to follow the example of Yao and the other ancient sage rulers who were said to have ceded the empire to worthy aides. He voluntarily turned over the throne of Yan to his prime minister, and in no time the state was torn by internal strife and had fallen prey to invaders. Perhaps Xunzi had this fiasco in mind when he took up his brush to denounce the exponents of the ceding legend.

and far worse, it followed Qin custom in enforcing the cruel "three sets of relatives" penalty, by which all the close kin of a major criminal were sentenced to death along with the offender himself, though Xunzi had denounced this barbarous practice as the mark of a degenerate age (sec. 24). Moreover, many of its thinkers, among them scholars of the Confucian school, turned their attention to the very speculations and magical practices which Xunzi had warned them away from; where Xunzi poked fun at rain-making ceremonies, the leading Confucian writer of the early Han, Dong Zhongshu, solemnly wrote a chapter on how to conduct them.

Nevertheless, many evidences of the healthy influence of Xunzi's thought are discernible in Han intellectual life. His rationalism and humanism are reflected in the work of men like the historians Sima Qian and Ban Gu, or the philosophers Yang Xiong and Wang Chong, and his strong emphasis upon education and the study of the Classics led to the founding of a state university and government support and encouragement of classical learning. Compared to later dynasties, the Han was in many respects a bloody and barbarous age, but without Xunzi's humanizing influence it might well have been darker still.

We have no way of telling when or where Xunzi wrote the various sections of his work, or what state the text was in at the time of his death. The first edition of his work was compiled by the Han court scholar Liu Xiang (77–6 B.C.), who states that he examined 322 *pian*—sections, or bundles of bamboo writing slips—and, after sorting out the duplicates and fitting together fragments, arrived at the present arrangement of the text in 32 sections. (Evidence of the fragmentary and faulty state of the text even after it had passed through Liu Xiang's hands may be noted in the parts I have translated.) It is doubtful whether all 32 sections are by Xunzi himself, though I see no reason to question the authenticity of the sections presented here. In addition, 10 *pian* of poems in the *fu* or rhyme-prose style by Xunzi are record-ed in the "Treatise on Literature" of the *History of the Former Han* (*Hanshu* 30), but except for one brief section of *fu* preserved in the *Xunzi* itself, these seem to have been lost long ago.

While the *Analects* and *Mencius* were provided with commen-taries by late Han scholars, the *Xunzi* unfortunately did not enjoy this attention until much later. The earliest commentary is by the Tang scholar Yang Liang, and it is upon his edition, preface dated A.D. 818, that all later texts of the work are based. Further information on the texts and commentaries utilized in my translation will be found at the end of this introduction.

Finally a word should be said about the form and style of Xunzi's work. With the spread of literacy and the increased in-terest in philosophical and technical literature that marked the late years of the Zhou, the art of prose advanced remarkably in organization, clarity, and subtlety of expression. Xunzi utilized these advances to the full. In the writings of the Mohist school he had examples of clear, well-ordered essays centered around a single theme, and it was this form which he chose for the large part of his own work, though a few sections are in anecdote form. From the Mohists, too, and from Mencius he adopted the practice of rounding off a paragraph or step in his argument with an appropriate quotation from the *Odes* or *Documents*, or some traditional saying. In the first few sections of his work the style tends to be rather choppy and aphoristic; but in others, such as those on Heaven or the nature of man, his arguments are much more carefully spelled out and closely knit, perhaps evi-dence that these sections were composed later in his life. Though he employs the balanced, rhythmic style common to the period, he avoids the monotony and repetitiousness that mar the Mohist writings, taking care to vary his sentence patterns and to devise new and interesting modes of expression. His work, in fact, stands second only to the *Zhuangzi* as a masterpiece of early Chinese expository writing. He deliberately eschewed the mystical thought of Zhuangzi, and with it he lost much of the wit and fantasy that put the *Zhuangzi* in a class by itself. But he substituted for these a dignity, sincerity, and orderliness of expression that are unrivaled in the ancient period. Much of the lasting influence of his thought is due not only to the appeal and soundness of his ideas, but to the clarity and elegance with which they are set forth.

A great deal of work was done on the *Xunzi* by Qing scholars, the results of which were admirably summed up in the edition and commentary published in 1891 by Wang Xianqian entitled *Xunzi jijie*. (It has recently been reprinted on the mainland with no date given.) This edition is the basis of my translation and except when I have indicated otherwise, the emendations and interpretations I have followed are taken from Wang's commentary. The other most valuable aid I have used is the modern-language Japanese translation of the *Xunzi* by Kanaya Osamu published in 1961–62 in the Iwanami bunko series. Kanaya has utilized earlier commentaries by Japanese scholars, notably the *Doku Junshi* (preface dated 1763) by Ogyū Sorai, and the *Junshi zōchū* (1820) by Kubo Ai, which were unknown to Wang Xianqian, as well as all the most important recent studies by Chinese and Japanese scholars. Among these the most important, which I have also consulted, are: *Xunzi bushi* and *Xunzi jiaobu* by Liu Shipei, included in the *Liu Shenshu xiansheng yishu* (1934; the former recently reprinted on the mainland, with no date); *Xunzhu dingbu* by Zhong Tai (1936); *Xunzi xinzheng* by Yu Xingwu (1937); *Xunzi jianshi* by Liang Qixiong (Beijing, 1956; a revised edition of the work by the same name published in 1936); and *Xunzi jiaozheng* by Ruan Tingzhuo (Taipei, 1959). Kanaya also states that he has consulted the *Duxunzi zhaji* by Dao Hongqing, and the *Xunzi jijie buzheng* by Long Yuchun, two works not available to me. In addition to Kanaya's translation, I have consulted the older Japanese translation by Hattori Unokichi in the Kanbun sōsho series (1922), which is far superior to that by Sasakawa Rinpū in the Kokuyaku kanbun taisei series (1920); the English translation by Homer H. Dubs, *The Works of Hsüntze* (1928), as well as his companion study, *Hsüntze: The Moulder of Ancient Confucianism* (1927); and the translation by J. J. L. Duyvendak of Section 22, "Hsün-tzu on the Rectification of Names," *T'oung Pao*, XXIII, 221–54. Also of importance is the *Concordance to Hsün Tzu*, Harvard–Yen-ching Institute Sinological Index Series, Supplement #22 (1950).

⫘ ENCOURAGING LEARNING

(Section 1)

The gentleman says: Learning should never cease. Blue comes from the indigo plant but is bluer than the plant itself. Ice is made of water but is colder than water ever is. A piece of wood as straight as a plumb line may be bent into a circle as true as any drawn with a compass and, even after the wood has dried, it will not straighten out again. The bending process has made it that way. Thus, if wood is pressed against a straightening board, it can be made straight; if metal is put to the grindstone, it can be sharpened; and if the gentleman studies widely and each day examines himself, his wisdom will become clear and his conduct be without fault. If you do not climb a high mountain, you will not comprehend the highness of the heavens; if you do not look down into a deep valley, you will not know the depth of the earth; and if you do not hear the words handed down from the ancient kings, you will not understand the greatness of learning. Children born among the Han or Yue people of the south and among the Mo barbarians of the north cry with the same voice at birth, but as they grow older they follow different customs. Education causes them to differ. The *Odes* says:

> Oh, you gentlemen,
> Do not be constantly at ease and rest!
> Quietly respectful in your posts,
> Love those who are correct and upright
> And the gods will hearken to you
> And aid you with great blessing.[1]

There is no greater godliness[2] than to transform yourself with the Way, no greater blessing than to escape misfortune.

I once tried spending the whole day in thought, but I found it of less value than a moment of study.[3] I once tried standing on tiptoe and gazing into the distance, but I found I could see much farther by climbing to a high place. If you climb to a high place and wave to someone, it is not as though your arm were any longer than usual, and yet people can see you from much farther away. If you shout down the wind, it is not as though your voice were any stronger than usual, and yet people can hear you much more clearly. Those who make use of carriages or horses may not be any faster walkers than anyone else, and yet they are able to travel a thousand *li*. Those who make use of boats may not know how to swim, and yet they manage to get across rivers. The gentleman is by birth no different from any other man; it is just that he is good at making use of things.

In the south there is a bird called the *meng* dove. It makes a nest out of feathers woven together with hair and suspends it

---

[1]"Lesser Odes," *Xiaoming*, Mao text no. 207. Here and elsewhere in quotations from the *Odes* and *Documents* I have for the most part followed the interpretations of Karlgren.

[2]Xunzi repeats the word *shen* (gods) from the ode, but gives it a humanistic interpretation, making it a moral quality of the good man; I have therefore translated it as "godliness."

[3]A paraphrase of Confucius's remark in *Analects* XV, 30.

from the tips of the reeds. But when the wind comes, the reeds break, the eggs are smashed, and the baby birds killed. It is not that the nest itself is faulty; the fault is in the thing it is attached to. In the west there is a tree called the *yegan*. Its trunk is no more than four inches tall and it grows on top of the high mountains, from whence it looks down into valleys a hundred fathoms deep. It is not a long trunk which affords the tree such a view, but simply the place where it stands. If pigweed grows up in the midst of hemp, it will stand up straight without propping. If white sand is mixed with mud, it too will turn black.[4] The root of a certain orchid is the source of the perfume called *zhi*, but if the root were to be soaked in urine, then no gentleman would go near it and no commoner would consent to wear it. It is not that the root itself is of an unpleasant quality; it is the fault of the thing it has been soaked in. Therefore a gentleman will take care in selecting the community he intends to live in, and will choose men of breeding for his companions. In this way he wards off evil and meanness, and draws close to fairness and right.

Every phenomenon that appears must have a cause. The glory or shame that come to a man are no more than the image of his virtue. Meat when it rots breeds worms; fish that is old and dry brings forth maggots. When a man is careless and lazy and forgets himself, that is when disaster occurs. The strong naturally bear up under weight; the weak naturally end up bound.[5] Evil and corruption in oneself invite the anger of others. If you lay sticks of identical shape on a fire, the flames will seek out the driest ones; if you level the ground to an equal smoothness, water will still seek out the dampest spot. Trees of the same species grow together; birds and beasts gather in herds; for all

---

[4] This sentence has been restored from quotations of *Xunzi* preserved in other texts.
[5] Following the interpretation of Liu Shipei.

things follow after their own kind. Where a target is hung up, arrows will find their way to it; where the forest trees grow thickest, the axes will enter. When a tree is tall and shady, birds will flock to roost in it; when vinegar turns sour, gnats will collect around it. So there are words that invite disaster and actions that call down shame. A gentleman must be careful where he takes his stand.

Pile up earth to make a mountain and wind and rain will rise up from it. Pile up water to make a deep pool and dragons will appear. Pile up good deeds to create virtue and godlike understanding will come of itself; there the mind of the sage will find completion. But unless you pile up little steps, you can never journey a thousand *li*; unless you pile up tiny streams, you can never make a river or a sea. The finest thoroughbred cannot travel ten paces in one leap, but the sorriest nag can go a ten days' journey. Achievement consists of never giving up. If you start carving and then give up, you cannot even cut through a piece of rotten wood; but if you persist without stopping, you can carve and inlay metal or stone. Earthworms have no sharp claws or teeth, no strong muscles or bones, and yet above ground they feast on the mud, and below they drink at the yellow springs. This is because they keep their minds on one thing. Crabs have six legs and two pincers, but unless they can find an empty hole dug by a snake or a water serpent, they have no place to lodge. This is because they allow their minds to go off in all directions. Thus if there is no dark and dogged will, there will be no shining accomplishment; if there is no dull and determined effort, there will be no brilliant achievement. He who tries to travel two roads at once will arrive nowhere; he who serves two masters will please neither. The wingless dragon has no limbs and yet it can soar; the flying squirrel has many talents but finds itself hard pressed. The *Odes* says:

> Ringdove in the mulberry,
> Its children are seven.
> The good man, the gentleman,
> His forms are one.
> His forms are one,
> His heart is as though bound.[6]

Thus does the gentleman bind himself to oneness.

In ancient times, when Hu Ba played the zither, the fish in the streams came forth to listen; when Bo Ya played the lute, the six horses of the emperor's carriage looked up from their feed trough. No sound is too faint to be heard, no action too well concealed to be known. When there are precious stones under the mountain, the grass and trees have a special sheen; where pearls grow in a pool, the banks are never parched. Do good and see if it does not pile up. If it does, how can it fail to be heard of?

Where does learning begin and where does it end? I say that as to program, learning begins with the recitation of the Classics and ends with the reading of the ritual texts; and as to objective, it begins with learning to be a man of breeding, and ends with learning to be a sage.[7] If you truly pile up effort over a long period of time, you will enter into the highest realm. Learning continues until death and only then does it cease. Therefore we may speak of an end to the program of learning, but the objective of learning must never for an instant be given up. To pursue it is to

---

[6]"Airs of Cao," *Shijiu*, Mao text no. 152. The last line I have interpreted differently from Karlgren in order to make it fit Xunzi's comment.

[7]Xunzi customarily distinguishes three grades in the moral hierarchy of men: *shi*, *junzi*, and *shengren*, which I have translated as "man of breeding," "gentleman," and "sage" respectively, though at times he uses the first two terms more or less interchangeably.

be a man, to give it up is to become a beast. The *Book of Documents* is the record of government affairs, the *Odes* the repository of correct sounds, and the rituals are the great basis of law and the foundation of precedents. Therefore learning reaches its completion with the rituals, for they may be said to represent the highest point of the Way and its power. The reverence and order of the rituals, the fitness and harmony of music, the breadth of the *Odes* and *Documents*, the subtlety of the *Spring and Autumn Annals*—these encompass all that is between heaven and earth.

The learning of the gentleman enters his ear, clings to his mind, spreads through his four limbs, and manifests itself in his actions. His smallest word, his slightest movement can serve as a model. The learning of the petty man enters his ear and comes out his mouth. With only four inches between ear and mouth, how can he have possession of it long enough to ennoble a seven-foot body? In old times men studied for their own sake; nowadays men study with an eye to others.[8] The gentleman uses learning to ennoble himself; the petty man uses learning as a bribe to win attention from others. To volunteer information when you have not been asked is called officiousness; to answer two questions when you have been asked only one is garrulity. Both officiousness and garrulity are to be condemned. The gentleman should be like an echo.

In learning, nothing is more profitable than to associate with those who are learned. Ritual and music present us with models but no explanations; the *Odes* and *Documents* deal with ancient matters and are not always pertinent; the *Spring and Autumn Annals* is terse and cannot be quickly understood. But if you make use of the erudition of others and the explanations of gentlemen, then you will become honored and may make your way any-

---

[8]This sentence is quoted from *Analects* XIV, 25, where it is attributed to Confucius.

where in the world. Therefore I say that in learning nothing is more profitable than to associate with those who are learned, and of the roads to learning, none is quicker than to love such men. Second only to this is to honor ritual. If you are first of all unable to love such men and secondly are incapable of honoring ritual, then you will only be learning a mass of jumbled facts, blindly following the *Odes* and *Documents*, and nothing more. In such a case you may study to the end of your days and you will never be anything but a vulgar pedant.[9] If you want to become like the former kings and seek out benevolence and righteousness, then ritual is the very road by which you must travel. It is like picking up a fur coat by the collar: grasp it with all five fingers and the whole coat can easily be lifted. To lay aside the rules of ritual and try to attain your objective with the *Odes* and *Documents* alone is like trying to measure the depth of a river with your finger, to pound millet with a spear point, or to eat a pot of stew with an awl. You will get nowhere. Therefore one who honors ritual, though he may not yet have full understanding, can be called a model man of breeding; while one who does not honor ritual, though he may have keen perception, is no more than a desultory pedant.

Do not answer a man whose questions are gross. Do not question a man whose answers are gross. Do not listen to a man whose theories are gross. Do not argue with a contentious man. Only if a man has arrived where he is by the proper way should you have dealings with him; if not, avoid him. If he is respectful in his person,[10] then you may discuss with him the approach to

---

[9]Literally, "vulgar Confucian," but here and below Xunzi uses the word *ru* in the older and broader sense of a scholar.
[10]Reading *ti* instead of *li* in order to complete the parallelism with "words" and "looks."

the Way. If his words are reasonable, you may discuss with him the principles of the Way. If his looks are gentle, you may discuss with him the highest aspects of the Way. To speak to someone you ought not to is called officiousness; to fail to speak to someone you ought to is called secretiveness; to speak to someone without first observing his temper and looks is called blindness.[11] The gentleman is neither officious, secretive, nor blind, but cautious and circumspect in his manner. This is what the *Odes* means when it says:

> Neither overbearing nor lax,
> They are rewarded by the Son of Heaven.[12]

He who misses one shot in a hundred cannot be called a really good archer; he who sets out on a thousand-mile journey and breaks down half a pace from his destination cannot be called a really good carriage driver; he who does not comprehend moral relationships and categories and who does not make himself one with benevolence and righteousness cannot be called a good scholar. Learning basically means learning to achieve this oneness. He who starts off in this direction one time and that direction another is only a commoner of the roads and alleys, while he who does a little that is good and much that is not good is no better than the tyrants Jie and Zhou or Robber Zhi.

The gentleman knows that what lacks completeness and purity does not deserve to be called beautiful. Therefore he reads and listens to explanations in order to penetrate the Way, ponders in

---

[11]This sentence is a paraphrase of *Analects* XVI, 6, where the saying is attributed to Confucius.

[12]"Lesser Odes," *Caishu*, Mao text no. 222. But Xunzi quotes from the Lu version, which differs slightly from the Mao text.

order to understand it, associates with men who embody it in order to make it part of himself, and shuns those who impede it in order to sustain and nourish it. He trains his eyes so that they desire only to see what is right, his ears so that they desire to hear only what is right, his mind so that it desires to think only what is right. When he has truly learned to love what is right, his eyes will take greater pleasure in it than in the five colors; his ears will take greater pleasure than in the five sounds; his mouth will take greater pleasure than in the five flavors; and his mind will feel keener delight than in the possession of the world. When he has reached this stage, he cannot be subverted by power or the love of profit; he cannot be swayed by the masses; he cannot be moved by the world. He follows this one thing in life; he follows it in death. This is what is called constancy of virtue. He who has such constancy of virtue can order himself, and, having ordered himself, he can then respond to others. He who can order himself and respond to others—this is what is called the complete man. It is the characteristic of heaven to manifest brightness, of earth to manifest breadth, and of the gentleman to value completeness.

When you see good, then diligently examine your own behavior; when you see evil, then with sorrow look into yourself. When you find good in yourself, steadfastly approve it; when you find evil in yourself, hate it as something loathsome. He who comes to you with censure is your teacher; he who comes with approbation is your friend; but he who flatters you is your enemy. Therefore the gentleman honors his teacher, draws close to his friends, but heartily hates his enemies. He loves good untiringly and can accept reprimand and take warning from it. Therefore, though he may have no particular wish to advance, how can he help but do so? The petty man is just the opposite. He behaves in an unruly way and yet hates to have others censure him; he does unworthy deeds and yet wants others to regard him as worthy. He has the heart of a tiger or a wolf, the actions of a beast, and yet resents it when others look upon him as an enemy. He draws close to those who flatter him and is distant with those who reprimand him; he laughs at upright men and treats as enemies those who are loyal. Therefore, though he certainly has no desire for ruin, how can he escape it? This is what is meant by the lines in the *Odes*:

They league together, they slander;
It fills me with sorrow.
When advice is good
They all oppose it.
When advice is bad,
They follow all together.[1]

This is the way with impartial goodness: use it to control your temperament and nourish your life and you will live longer than Pengzu;[2] use it to improve and strengthen[3] yourself and you may become equal to the sages Yao and Yu. It is appropriate when you are in a time of success; it is profitable when you are living in hardship. It is in fact what is meant by ritual. If all matters pertaining to temperament, will, and understanding proceed according to ritual, they will be ordered and successful; if not they will be perverse and violent or slovenly and rude. If matters pertaining to food and drink, dress, domicile, and living habits proceed according to ritual, they will be harmonious and well regulated; if not they will end in missteps, excesses, and sickness. If matters pertaining to deportment, attitude, manner of movement, and walk proceed according to ritual, they will be refined; if not they will be arrogant and uncouth, common and countrified. Therefore a man without ritual cannot live; an undertaking without ritual cannot come to completion; a state without ritual cannot attain peace. This is what is meant by the lines in the *Odes*:

Their rites and ceremonies are entirely according to rule,
Their laughter and talk are entirely appropriate.[4]

---

[1]"Lesser Odes," *Xiaomin*, Mao text no. 195.
[2]An ancient worthy supposed to have lived for seven hundred years.
[3]Reading *jiang* instead of *ming*.
[4]"Lesser Odes," *Chuci*, Mao text no. 209.

To make use of good to lead others is called education; to make use of good to achieve harmony with others is called amenity. To use what is not good to lead others is called betrayal; to use what is not good to achieve harmony with others is called sycophancy. To treat right as right and wrong as wrong is called wisdom; to treat right as wrong and wrong as right is called stupidity. To speak ill of good men is called slander; to do harm to good men is called brigandage. To call right right and wrong wrong is called honesty. To steal goods is called robbery; to act on the sly is called deceit; to go back on your word is called perfidy. To be without a fixed standard in your actions is called inconstancy. To cling to profit and cast aside righteousness is called the height of depravity. He who has heard much is called broad; he who has heard little is called shallow. He who has seen much is called practiced; he who has seen little is called uncouth. He who has difficulty advancing is called a laggard; he who forgets easily is called a leaky-brain. He whose actions are few and well principled is called orderly; he whose actions are many and disorderly is called chaotic.

This is the proper way to order the temperament and train the mind. If your temperament is too strong and stubborn, soften it with harmony. If your intellect is too deep and withdrawn, unify it with mild sincerity. If you are too courageous and fierce, correct the fault with orderly compliance. If you are too hasty and flippant, regulate the fault with restraint. If you are too constrained and petty, broaden yourself with liberality. If you are too low-minded, lethargic, and greedy, lift yourself up with high ambitions. If you are mediocre, dull, and diffuse, strip away your failings by means of teachers and friends. If you are indolent and heedless, awaken yourself with the thought of imminent disaster. If you are stupidly sincere and ploddingly honest, temper your character with rites and music.[5] Of all the ways to order the temperament and train the mind, none is more direct than to follow ritual, none more vital than to find a teacher, none more godlike than to learn to love one thing alone. This is called the proper way to order the temperament and train the mind.

If your will is well disciplined, you may hold up your head before wealth and eminence; if you are rich in righteous ways, you may stand unmoved before kings and dukes. Look well inside yourself and you may look lightly upon outside things. This is what the old text[6] means when it says, "The gentleman uses things; the petty man is used by things." Though it may mean labor for the body, if the mind finds peace in it, do it. Though there may be little profit in it, if there is much righteousness, do it. Rather than achieve success in the service of an unprincipled ruler, it is better to follow what is right in the service of an impoverished one. A good farmer does not give up plowing just because of flood or drought; a good merchant does not stop doing business just because of occasional losses; a gentleman does not neglect the Way just because of poverty and hardship.

If you are respectful in bearing and sincere in heart, if you abide by ritual principles and are kindly to others, then you may travel all over the world and, though you may choose to live among the barbarian tribes, everyone will honor you. If you are the first to undertake hard work and can leave ease and enjoyment to others, if you are honest and trustworthy, persevering, and meticulous in your job, then you can travel all over the world and, though you choose to live among the barbarians, everyone

---

[5]I have omitted five characters which destroy the balance of the sentence and do not seem to belong here.

[6]*Zhuan*, the general term for a text or saying handed down from former times. It is impossible to identify the source of such quotations in Xunzi.

will want to employ you. But if your bearing is arrogant and your heart deceitful, if you follow dark and injurious ways[7] and are inconsistent and vile in feeling, then you may travel all over the world and, though you penetrate to every corner of it, there will be no one who does not despise you. If you are shiftless and evasive when it comes to hard work but keen and unrestrained in the pursuit of pleasure, if you are dishonest and insincere, concerned only with your own desires[8] and unattentive to your work, then you may travel all over the world and, though you penetrate to every corner of it, there will be no one who does not reject you.

One does not walk with his arms held out like wings because he is afraid of soiling his sleeves in the mud.[9] One does not walk with his head bent down because he is afraid of bumping into something. One does not lower his eyes when meeting others because he is overcome with fright. It is simply that a man of breeding desires to improve his conduct by himself and to cause no offense to his neighbors.

A thoroughbred can travel a thousand *li* in one day, yet even a tired old nag, given ten days to do it in, can cover the same distance. But will you try to exhaust the inexhaustible, to pursue to the end that which has no end? If you do, then you may wear out your bones and flesh but you will never reach your goal. If, however, you set a limit to your journey, then you may arrive there sooner or later, before others or after them, but how can you fail to arrive at your goal some time? Will you be an unwitting plodder who tries to exhaust the inexhaustible, to pursue to the end that which has no end? Or will you choose to set a limit to your

---

[7]Following the interpretation of Liu Shipei. The older interpretation is "if you follow the ways of Shen Dao [a Daoist Legalist thinker] and Mozi."

[8]Following the interpretation of Liu Shipei.

[9]Compare the description of Confucius in *Analects* X, 3: "He hastened forward, with his arms like the wings of a bird."

journey? It is not that the propositions concerning black and white, sameness and difference, thickness and non-thickness are not penetrating.[10] But the gentleman does not discuss them because he puts a limit to his goal. Therefore in learning there is what is called "waiting." If those who have gone before stop and wait, and those who are behind keep going, then, whether sooner or later, whether first or last, how can they fail all in time to reach the goal? If he keeps putting one foot in front of the other without stopping, even a lame turtle can go a thousand *li*; if you keep piling up one handful of earth on top of another without ceasing, you will end up with a high mountain. But if you block the source of a river and break down its banks, even the Yangzi and the Yellow River can be made to run dry; if they take one step forward and one step back, pull now to the left and now to the right, even a team of six thoroughbreds will never reach their destination. Men are certainly not as widely separated in their capacities as a lame turtle and a team of six thoroughbreds; yet the lame turtle reaches the goal where the team of thoroughbreds fails. There is only one reason: one keeps on going, the other does not. Though the road is short, if you do not step along you will never get to the end; though the task is small, if you do not work at it you will never get it finished. He who takes many holidays will never excel others by very much.[11]

He who loves law and puts it into effect is a man of breeding. He who has a firm will and embodies it in his conduct is a gentleman. He who has a keen insight which never fails is a sage.

---

[10]These were among the favorite paradoxes or topics of logical debate propounded by Hui Shi, Gongsun Long, and other philosophers of the School of Names. Though Xunzi learned much from these men, he scorned the discussion of logic for its own sake.

[11]Reading *ren* instead of *ru*.

A man who has no laws at all is lost and guideless. A man who has laws but does not understand their meaning is timid and inconsistent. Only if a man abides by laws and at the same time comprehends their wider significance and applicability can he become truly liberal and compassionate.

Ritual is the means by which to rectify yourself; the teacher is the means by which ritual is rectified. If you are without ritual, how can you rectify yourself? If you have no teacher, how can you understand the fitness of ritual? If you unerringly do as ritual prescribes, it means that your emotions have found rest in ritual. If you speak as your teacher speaks, it means that your understanding has become like that of your teacher. If your emotions find rest in ritual and your understanding is like that of your teacher, then you have become a sage. Hence to reject ritual is to be without law and to reject your teacher is to be without a guide. To deny guide and law and attempt to do everything your own way is to be like a blind man trying to distinguish colors or a deaf man, tones. Nothing will come of it but confusion and outrage. Therefore learning means learning to regard ritual as your law. The teacher makes himself the standard of proper conduct and values that in himself which finds rest in ritual. This is what is meant by the lines in the *Odes*:

> Without considering, without thinking,
> He obeys the laws of God.[12]

If a man is sincere, obedient, and brotherly, he may be said to have a certain amount of good in him. But if he adds to this a love of learning, modesty, and alertness, then[13] he may be considered

---

[12]"Greater Odes," *Huangyi*, Mao text no. 241.

[13]Omitting the four characters that follow, which do not seem to belong here.

a gentleman. If a man is mean and lazy, lacking in modesty, and a glutton over food and drink, he may be said to have a certain amount of bad in him. But if in addition he is wanton, reckless, and disobedient, vicious and evil and lacking in brotherly feeling, then he can be called ill-omened,[14] and no one can protest if he falls into the hands of the law and is executed.

If you treat old people as they ought to be treated, then young people too will come to your side. If you do not press those who are already hard pressed, then the successful too will gather around you. If you do good in secret and seek no reward for your kindness, then sages and unworthy men alike will be with you. If a man does these three things, though he should commit a grave error, will Heaven leave him to perish?

The gentleman is careless in the pursuit of profit but swift in avoiding harm. Timidly he shuns disgrace but he practices the principles of the Way with courage.

Though poor and hard pressed, a gentleman will be broad of will. Though rich and eminent, he will be respectful in his manner. Though at ease, he will not allow his spirit to grow indolent; though weary, he will not neglect his appearance. He will not take away more than is right because of anger, nor give more than is right because of joy. Though poor and hard pressed, he is broad of will because he honors benevolence. Though rich and eminent, he is respectful in manner because he does not presume upon his station. Though at ease, he is not indolent because he chooses to follow what is right. Though weary, he does not neglect his appearance because he values good form.[15] He does not take away too much in anger nor give too much in joy because he allows law to prevail over personal feeling. The *Book*

---

[14]Omitting the *shao*, a contamination from the sentence above.

[15]Reading *wen* instead of *jiao*.

of Documents says: "Do not go by what you like, but follow the way of the king; do not go by what you hate, but follow the king's road."[16] This means that a gentleman must be able to suppress personal desire in favor of public right.

---

[16]Documents of Zhou, *Hongfan* or "Great Plan."

Someone asked how to govern, and I replied: In the case of worthy and able men, promote them without waiting for their turn to come up. In the case of inferior and incompetent men, dismiss them without hesitation. In the case of incorrigibly evil men, punish them without trying to reform them.[1] In the case of people of average capacity, teach them what is right without attempting to force them into goodness. Thus, even where rank has not yet been fixed, the distinction between good and bad will be as clear as that between the left and right ancestors in the mortuary temple.[2] Although a man may be the descendant of

---

[1]This recognition of a category of incorrigibly bad men seems to contradict the rest of Xunzi's philosophy and is rare in early Confucian thought as a whole. Nevertheless, Xunzi refers to it elsewhere, as in sec. 18, where he argues that the existence of a very few such perverse and unteachable men even in the time of a sage ruler is not to be taken as evidence that the ruler himself is at fault.

[2]This sentence has long puzzled commentators, and the translation is tentative. According to Zhou practice, the mortuary temple of the founder of a noble family was placed in the center, with the temples of the second, fourth, and sixth descendants ranged to the left and called *zhao*, while those of the third, fifth, and seventh descendants were ranged to the right and called *mu*.

kings, dukes, or high court ministers, if he cannot adhere to ritual principles, he should be ranked among the commoners. Although a man may be the descendant of commoners, if he has acquired learning, is upright in conduct, and can adhere to ritual principles, he should be promoted to the post of prime minister or high court official. When it comes to men of perverse words and theories, perverse undertakings and talents, or to people who are slippery or vagrant, they should be given tasks to do, taught what is right, and allowed a period of trial. Encourage them with rewards, discipline them with punishments, and if they settle down to their work, then look after them as subjects; but if not, cast them out. In the case of those who belong to the five incapacitated groups,[3] the government should gather them together, look after them, and give them whatever work they are able to do. Employ them, provide them with food and clothing, and take care to see that none are left out. If anyone is found acting or using his talents to work against the good of the time, condemn him to death without mercy. This is what is called the virtue of Heaven and the government of a true king.

These are the essential points to remember when listening to proposals in government. If a man comes forward in good faith, treat him according to ritual; if he comes forward in bad faith, meet him with punishment. In this way the two categories will be clearly distinguished, worthy and unworthy men will not be thrown together, and right and wrong will not be confused. If worthy and unworthy men are not thrown together, then men of extraordinary character will come to you, and if right and wrong are not confused, then the nation will be well ordered. This accomplished, your fame will increase each day, the world

---

[3]Defined by commentators as those who are dumb, deaf, crippled, missing an arm or leg, or dwarfed.

will look to you with longing, your orders will be carried out, your prohibitions heeded, and you will have fulfilled all the duties of a king.

In listening to reports and proposals, if you are too stern and severe and have no patience in guiding and drawing others out, then your subordinates will be fearful and distant and will withdraw into themselves and be unwilling to speak. In such a case important matters are likely to be left unattended to and minor matters to be botched. If, however, you are too sympathetic and understanding, too fond of leading and drawing others out, and have no sense of where to stop, then men will come with all sorts of perverse suggestions and you will be flooded with dubious proposals. In such a case you will find yourself with too much to listen to and too much to do, and this also will be inimical to good government.

If there are laws, but in actual practice they do not prove to be of general applicability, then points not specifically covered by the laws are bound to be left undecided. If men are appointed to posts but they have no overall understanding of their duties, then matters which do not specifically fall within their jurisdiction are bound to be neglected. Therefore there must be laws that prove applicable in practice and men in office who have an overall understanding of their duties. There must be no hidden counsels or overlooked ability on the lower levels and all matters must proceed without error. Only a gentleman is capable of such government.

Fair-mindedness is the balance in which to weigh proposals;[4] upright harmoniousness is the line by which to measure them. Where laws exist, to carry them out; where they do not exist, to act in the spirit of precedent and analogy—this is the

---

[4]Reading *ting* instead of *zhi*.

best way to hear proposals. To show favoritism and partisan feeling and be without any constant principles—this is the worst you can do. It is possible to have good laws and still have disorder in the state. But to have a gentleman acting as ruler and disorder in the state—from ancient times to the present I have never heard of such a thing. This is what the old text means when it says, "Order is born from the gentleman, disorder from the petty man."

Where ranks are all equal, there will not be enough goods to go around; where power is equally distributed, there will be a lack of unity; where there is equality among the masses, it will be impossible to employ them. The very existence of Heaven and Earth exemplifies the principle of higher and lower, but only when an enlightened king appears on the throne can the nation be governed according to regulation. Two men of equal eminence cannot govern each other; two men of equally humble station cannot employ each other. This is the rule of Heaven. If men are of equal power and station and have the same likes and dislikes, then there will not be enough goods to supply their wants and they will inevitably quarrel. Quarreling must lead to disorder, and disorder to exhaustion. The former kings abhorred such disorder and therefore they regulated the principles of ritual in order to set up ranks. They established the distinctions between rich and poor, eminent and humble, making it possible for those above to join together and watch over those below. This is the basis upon which the people of the world are nourished. This is what the *Documents* means when it says, "Equality is based upon inequality."[5]

_____

[5] I take it that this is the way Xunzi, quoting very much out of context, wishes us to understand these four characters. In context, in the section called *Lüxing* or "The Code of Marquis Lü," they have a quite different meaning.

If the horses are frightened of the carriage, then the gentleman cannot ride in safety; if the common people are frightened of the government, then the gentleman cannot occupy his post in safety. If the horses are frightened of the carriage, the best thing to do is to quiet them; if the common people are frightened of the government, the best thing to do is to treat them with kindness. Select men who are worthy and good for government office, promote those who are kind and respectful, encourage filial piety and brotherly affection, look after orphans and widows and assist the poor, and then the common people will feel safe and at ease with their government. And once the common people feel safe, then the gentleman may occupy his post in safety. This is what the old text means when it says, "The ruler is the boat and the common people are the water. It is the water that bears the boat up, and the water that capsizes it." Therefore, if the gentleman desires safety, the best thing for him to do is to govern fairly and to love the people. If he desires glory, the best thing is to honor ritual and treat men of breeding with respect. If he desires to win fame and merit, the best thing is to promote the worthy and employ men of ability. These are the three great obligations of the ruler. If he meets these three, then all other obligations will likewise be met; if he does not meet these three, then, although he manages to meet his other obligations, it will scarcely be of any benefit to him. Confucius has said, "If he meets both his major and minor obligations correctly, he is a superior ruler. If he meets his major obligations but is inconsistent in meeting his minor ones, he is a mediocre ruler. If he fails to meet his major obligations, though he may meet his minor ones correctly enough, I do not care to see any more of him."

Marquis Cheng and Lord Si were rulers who knew how to collect taxes and keep accounts, but they did not succeed in winning the support of the people.[6] Zichan won the support of the people but did not succeed in governing them.[7] Guan Zhong governed the state but did not get around to promoting ritual.[8] He who promotes ritual will become a true king; he who governs well will be strong; he who wins over the people will find safety; but he who pays attention only to the collection of taxes will be lost. Thus, a king enriches his people, a dictator enriches his soldiers, a state that is barely managing to survive enriches its high officers, and a doomed state enriches only its coffers and stuffs its storehouses. But if its coffers are heaped up and its storehouses full, while its people are impoverished, this is what is called to overflow at the top but dry up at the bottom. Such a state will be unable to protect itself at home and unable to fight its enemies abroad, and its downfall and destruction can be looked for at any moment. The ruler of such a state, by col-

---

[6]Two rulers of the state of Wei (the small state northwest of Qi, not to be confused with the much more powerful state in the old territory of Jin whose name is also read "Wei") in the late fourth century B.C. As the state of Wei dwindled in size and power, its rulers voluntarily downgraded themselves from the title of duke to marquis, and later from marquis to lord.

[7]Chief minister of the small state of Zheng in the 6th century B.C. (The *Zuozhuan* records his death in 522 B.C.) He was widely praised for his wise and benevolent policies, especially by Confucius (see *Analects* V, 15). But Xunzi here follows the more reserved estimation of Mencius (*Mencius* IVB, 2): "Zichan . . . was kind but did not understand how to govern."

[8]Chief minister to Duke Huan of Qi in the 7th century B.C. and a well-known figure in history and legend. According to *Shiji* 32, he died in 645 B.C. The philosophic work known as *Guanzi* is said to embody his teachings on economics and statecraft. He is credited with having made Duke Huan the first of the *ba* (overlords, dictators, or hegemons). Xunzi, like all early Confucian writers, distinguishes carefully between the *wang*, the true kings who qualify for their position by virtue and public sanction and who conduct their government on the basis of correct ritual principles, and the *ba*, feudal lords who, by strengthening their military and economic power and overawing the other feudal lords, were for a time able to dictate to the empire and even force a kind of recognition from the Zhou king.

lecting excessive taxes, brings about his own destruction, and his enemies, by seizing his territory, make themselves stronger than ever. Too much attention to tax collecting invites bandits and fattens one's enemies. It is the path which leads to the destruction of the state and the peril of its lord, and for that reason the enlightened ruler does not follow it.

The king works to acquire men, the dictator works to acquire allies, and the ruler who relies on force works to acquire territory. He who acquires men wins the allegiance of the feudal lords; he who acquires allies wins the friendship of the feudal lords; but he who acquires territory incurs their enmity. He who commands the allegiance of the feudal lords may become a king; he who wins their friendship may become a dictator; but he who incurs their enmity is in danger.

He who lives by force must use his might to conquer the cities that other men guard and to defeat the soldiers[9] that other men send forth to battle, and in doing so he inevitably inflicts great injury upon the people of other states. If he inflicts great injury upon them, they will inevitably hate him fiercely and will day by day grow more eager to fight against him. Moreover, he who uses his might to conquer the cities that other men guard and to defeat the soldiers that other men send forth to battle must inevitably inflict great injury upon his own people as well. If he inflicts great injury upon his own people, they will inevitably hate him fiercely and will day by day grow less eager to fight his battles. With the people of other states growing daily more eager to fight against him, and his own people growing daily less eager to fight in his defense, the ruler who relies upon strength will on the contrary be reduced to weakness. He acquires territory but loses the support of his people; his worries

---

[9]Reading *shi* instead of *chu* here and in the parallel sentence below.

increase while his accomplishments dwindle. He finds himself with more and more cities to guard and less and less of the means to guard them with; thus in time the great state will on the contrary be stripped down in this way to insignificance. The other feudal lords never cease to eye him with hatred and to dream of revenge;[10] never do they forget their enmity. They spy out his weak points and take advantage of his defects, so that he lives in constant peril.

One who truly understands how to use force[11] does not rely upon force. He is careful to follow the commands of the nominal king, builds up his might, and creates a fund of good will.[12] With his might well established, he cannot be weakened by the other feudal lords; with a fund of good will to rely on, he cannot be reduced to insignificance by the other feudal lords. Thus, if he happens to live in a time when there is no true king or dictator in the world, he will always be victorious. This is the way of one who truly understands how to use force.

The dictator is not like this. He opens up lands for cultivation, fills the granaries, and sees that the people are provided with the goods they need. He is careful in selecting his officials and employs men of talent, leading them on with rewards and correcting them with punishments. He restores states that have perished, protects ruling lines that are in danger of dying out, guards the weak, and restrains the violent. If he shows no intention of annexing the territories of his neighbors, then the other feudal lords will draw close to him. If he treats them as friends

---

[10]Following the interpretation of Liu Shipei.

[11]Reading *dao* instead of *da*.

[12]Xunzi says, literally, "establishes his virtue." But it is clear that he is using the word *de* (virtue), not in the higher ethical sense, but in the sense of favors or good turns done to others which put them in debt to one.

and equals and is respectful in his dealings with them, he will win their favor. He can win their intimacy by not attempting to annex them, but if he shows any inclination to annex their lands, they will turn away from him. He can win their favor by treating them as friends and equals, but if he shows any inclination to treat them as subjects, they will reject him. Therefore he makes it clear from his actions that he does not wish to annex their territory, and inspires faith in them that he will always treat them as friends and equals. Thus, if he happens to live in a time when there is no true king[13] in the world, he will always be victorious. This is the way of one who truly understands how to be a dictator. The reason that King Min of Qi was defeated by the armies of the five states, and that Duke Huan of Qi was threatened by Duke Zhuang of Lu was none other than this: they did not follow the way appropriate to their own positions, but tried to act in the manner of a true king.[14]

The true king is not like this. His benevolence is the loftiest in the world, his righteousness is the loftiest in the world, and his authority is the loftiest in the world. Since his benevolence is the loftiest in the world, there is no one in the world who does not draw close to him. Since his righteousness is the loftiest in the world, there is no one who does not respect him. Since his authority is the loftiest in the world, there is no one who dares to oppose him. With an authority that cannot be opposed, abetted

[13]Omitting the *ba*, which is clearly superfluous here.
[14]In 285 B.C., according to *Shiji* 46, King Min, who had aroused the anger of the other feudal lords, was attacked by a combination of them and driven from his capital. In 681 B.C., Duke Huan of Qi, the first of the *ba* or dictators, called the other feudal lords to a conference in Qi. According to what is probably a late legend, recorded in the *Gongyang Commentary* (Duke Zhuang 13), the general of Duke Zhuang of Lu managed to threaten Duke Huan with assassination and force him to return to Lu the territory which he had earlier seized.

by ways which win men's allegiance, he gains victory without battle and acquires territory without attack. He need not wear out his men and arms, and yet the whole world is won over to him. This is the way of one who understands how to be a king. He who understands these three ways may choose to become a king, a dictator, or a man of force as he wishes.

These are the king's regulations: they do not seek to pattern themselves on anything earlier than the Three Dynasties,[15] they do not reject the model of later kings. Seeking a pattern in the age before the Three Dynasties will lead to confusion; rejecting the model of later kings will lead to inelegance. Clothing should be of a fixed type, dwellings of fixed size, and servants and followers of fixed number. Likewise, the vessels and trappings used in mourning and sacrifice should all be fixed in accordance with social rank. All music that is lacking in classical elegance should be abandoned; all decorations that do not follow old patterns should be given up; all vessels and trappings that are not like those of earlier times should be discarded. This is what is called reviving the old. These are the king's regulations.

These are the judgments of a king: no man of virtue shall be left unhonored; no man of ability shall be left unemployed; no man of merit shall be left unrewarded; no man of guilt shall be left unpunished. No man by luck alone shall attain a position at court; no man by luck alone shall make his way among the people. The worthy shall be honored, the able employed, and each shall be assigned to his appropriate position without oversight. The violent[16] shall be repressed, the evil restrained, and punishments shall be meted out without error. The common people

---

[15]The Xia, Shang or Yin, and Zhou dynasties. By Xunzi's time the Zhou dynasty was regarded as extinct in all but name.
[16]Reading *bao* instead of *yuan*.

will then clearly understand that, if they do evil in secret, they will suffer punishment in public. This is what is called having fixed judgments. These are the king's judgments.

These are the king's laws.[17] They fix the various rates of taxation, regulate all affairs, exploit the ten thousand things, and thereby provide nourishment for all people. The tax on the fields shall be one tenth. At barriers and in markets, the officials shall examine the goods but levy no tax. The mountains, forests, lakes, and fish weirs shall at certain seasons be closed and at others opened for use, but no taxes shall be levied on their resources. Lands shall be inspected and the amount of tax graded according to their productivity. The distance over which articles of tribute must be transported shall be taken into consideration and the amount of tribute fixed accordingly. Goods and grain shall be allowed to circulate freely, so that there is no hindrance or stagnation in distribution; they shall be transported from one place to another as the need may arise, so that the entire region within the four seas becomes like one family. Thus those close to the king will not hide their talents or be stinted in their labors, and all regions, even the most distant and out of the way, will hasten to serve him and find peace and joy under his rule. This is what is called being the leader of men. These are the king's laws.

In the far north there are fast horses and howling dogs; China acquires and breeds them and puts them to work. In the far south there are feathers, tusks, hides, pure copper, and cinnabar; China acquires them and uses them in its manufactures. In the far east there are plants with purple dye, coarse hemp, fish, and salt; China acquires them for its food and clothing. In the far west there are skins and colored yaks' tails; China acquires them

---

[17]Supplying the word *fa* from the end of the paragraph.

for its needs. Thus the people living in lake regions have plenty of lumber and those living in the mountains have plenty of fish. The farmers do not have to carve or chisel, to fire or forge, and yet they have all the tools and utensils they need; the artisans and merchants do not have to work the fields, and yet they have plenty of vegetables and grain. The tiger and leopard are fierce beasts, but the gentleman strips off their hides for his personal use. Thus, wherever the sky stretches and the earth extends, there is nothing beautiful left unfound, nothing useful left unused. Such goods serve above to adorn worthy and good men, and below to nourish the common people and bring them security and happiness. This is what is called a state of godlike order. The *Odes* refers to this when it says:

> Heaven made a high hill;
> Tai Wang opened it up.
> He began the work
> And King Wen dwelt there in peace.[18]

One starts with general categories and moves to particular ones; one starts with unity and moves to plurality. What begins must end; what ends must begin again; and so the cycle repeats itself without interruption. Abandon this principle, and the empire will fall into decay. Heaven and earth are the beginning of life, ritual principles are the beginning of order, and the gentleman is the beginning of ritual principles. Acting on them, practicing them, guarding them, and loving them more than anything else—this is the beginning of the gentleman. Therefore Heaven and earth produce the gentleman and the gentleman

---

[18]"Hymns of Zhou," *Tianzuo*, Mao text no. 270. The high hill is Mount Qi, where Tai Wang, the ancestor of the Zhou royal family, built his capital.

brings order to Heaven and earth. The gentleman forms a triad *triad* with Heaven and earth; he is the controller of all things, the father and mother of the people. Without the gentleman, Heaven and earth will lack order and ritual principles will lack unity. There will be no true ruler or leader above, no true father or son below. This is what is called the extreme of chaos. The correct relationships between ruler and subject, father and son, elder and younger brother, and husband and wife begin and are carried through to the end, end and begin again. They share the order of Heaven and earth, they last for ten thousand generations. They are what is called the great foundation. The rules that govern mourning and sacrificial rites and the ceremonies of the court and army are based upon this single foundation. Those which guide the ruler in honoring or humbling, punishing or freeing, giving or taking from his subjects are based upon this unity. Those which teach men how to treat rulers as rulers, subjects as subjects, fathers as fathers, sons as sons, elder brothers as elder brothers, younger brothers as younger brothers are based upon this unity. Those which make a farmer a farmer, a man of breeding a man of breeding, an artisan an artisan, and a merchant a merchant are based upon this unity.

Fire and water possess energy but are without life. Grass and trees have life but no intelligence. Birds and beasts have intelligence but no sense of duty.[19] Man possesses energy, life, intelligence, and, in addition, a sense of duty. Therefore he is the noblest being on earth. He is not as strong as the ox, nor as swift as the horse, and yet he makes the ox and the horse work for him. Why? Because he is able to organize himself in society and they are not. Why is he able to organize himself in society? Because he sets up hierarchical divisions. And how is he able to set

---

[19]*Yi.* Elsewhere I have translated this word as righteousness.

up hierarchical divisions? Because he has a sense of duty. If he employs this sense of duty to set up hierarchical divisions, then there will be harmony. Where there is harmony there will be unity; where there is unity there will be strength; and where there is strength there will be the power to conquer all things. Thus men can dwell in security in their houses and halls. The reason that men are able to harmonize their actions with the order of the seasons, utilize all things, and bring universal profit to the world is simply this: they have established hierarchical divisions and possess a sense of duty.

Men, once born, must organize themselves into a society. But if they form a society without hierarchical divisions, then there will be quarreling. Where there is quarreling, there will be chaos; where there is chaos, there will be fragmentation; and where there is fragmentation, men will find themselves too weak to conquer other beings. Thus they will be unable to dwell in security in their houses and halls. This is why I say that ritual principles must not be neglected even for a moment. He who can follow them in serving his parents is called filial; he who can follow them in serving his elder brothers is called brotherly. He who can follow them in serving his superiors is called obedient; he who can follow them in employing his inferiors is called a ruler.

The ruler is one who is good at organizing men in society.[20] When society is properly organized, then all things will find their proper place, the six domestic animals[21] will breed and flourish, and all living beings will fulfill their allotted span of life. If breeding and tending is done at the proper time, the six domestic animals will increase. If planting and cutting is done at the proper time, plants and trees will flourish. If government

---

[20]Xunzi is here punning on the words *jun* (ruler) and *qun* (to form a group).

[21]Horses, cows, sheep, pigs, dogs, and chickens. Dogs were raised to be eaten.

commands are issued at the proper time, then the common people will be unified, and worthy and good men will offer their services. These are the regulations of a sage king.

When plants and trees are flowering or putting out new growth, no axes may be taken into the hills and forests, for they would destroy life and injure the growing things. When fish and other water creatures are breeding, no nets or poisons may be used in the lakes, for they would destroy life and injure the growing things. The farmers plow in spring, weed in summer, reap in fall, and store away in winter. Because they do each at the proper season, there is a never-ending supply of grain and the people have more than enough to eat. Because the lakes and rivers are watched over carefully and closed off at the proper time, there is an ever-increasing supply of fish and other water creatures and the people have more than they can use. Because the felling of trees and cutting of brush is done only at the proper time, the hills are never denuded and yet the people have all the wood they need. These are the measures of a sage king. He looks up to examine heaven, looks down to direct the work of the earth, completes all that is necessary between heaven and earth, and applies his action to all things. His actions are dark and yet of bright result, brief and yet long-lasting, narrow and yet broad. His understanding is of godlike clarity and breadth, and yet of the finest simplicity. Therefore it is said, he whose every move is founded on unity is a sage.[22]

The list of officials. The master of titles shall have charge of matters pertaining to the reception of guests, religious ceremonies, banquets, and sacrifices. The minister of the interior

---

[22]The end of this paragraph is couched in highly mysterious language and the translation, particularly of the last sentence, is tentative. Commentators offer various suggestions for amending the text, but none seems convincing enough to adopt.

shall have charge of matters pertaining to clan regulations, the walling of cities, and the standardization of utensils. The minister of war shall have charge of matters pertaining to military expeditions, weapons, carriages, and troop divisions.

To enforce the ordinances and commands, examine songs and writings, and abolish licentious music, attending to all matters at the appropriate time, so that strange and barbaric music is not allowed to confuse the elegant classical modes—these are the duties of the chief director of music. To repair dikes and weirs, open up canals and irrigation ditches, and cause water to flow freely and to be stored up properly in the reservoirs, opening or closing the sluice gates at the appropriate time, so that even in times of bad weather, flood, or drought, the people have fields that can be planted—these are the duties of the minister of works. To inspect the elevation of the fields, determine the fertility of the soil, decide what type of grain should be planted, examine the harvest and see that it is properly stored away, attending to all matters at the appropriate time, so that the farmers remain honest and hardworking and do not turn to other occupations—these are the duties of the administrator of the fields. To enforce the laws pertaining to the burning off of forests, and to conserve the resources of the mountains and woods, the marshes and lakes, such as trees, shrubs, fish, turtles, and various edible plants, attending to all matters at the appropriate time, so that the nation has the articles it needs and no resources are depleted—these are the duties of the director of resources. To order the provinces and communities, fix the regulations pertaining to dwellings, promote the raising of domestic animals and the planting of trees, encourage moral education, and promote filial piety and brotherly affection, attending to all matters at the appropriate time, so that the people are obedient to commands and live in their communities in security and happiness—

these are the duties of the director of communities. To judge the merits of the various artisans, determine the most appropriate time for their work, judge the quality of their manufactures, encourage efficiency and high quality, and see that all necessary goods are available, making sure that no one dares to manufacture sculptured or ornamented decorations privately at home— these are the duties of the director of artisans. To observe the yin and yang, judge the meaning of portents, divine by the tortoise and milfoil, conduct exorcisms, fortune-telling, and divination by the five types of signs, and understand all that pertains to good and bad fortune—these are the duties of hunchback shamanesses and crippled shamans. To attend to affairs of public sanitation, keep the roads in repair, eliminate thieves and highway bandits, insure a fair assignment of public buildings and market stalls,[23] attending to all matters at the appropriate time, so that traveling merchants can conduct their business in safety and there is an unobstructed flow of goods—these are the duties of the director of markets. To forestall violence and cruelty, prevent licentiousness, and wipe out evil, employing the five punishments[24] as a warning, causing the violent and cruel to change their ways and the wicked to desist from wickedness—these are the duties of the minister of justice.

To lay the foundation of governmental education, see that the laws and regulations are upright, receive reports and proposals and review them at fixed times, judge the merits of the lesser officials, and decide what rewards or punishments are to be meted out, attending to all matters carefully and at the proper time, so that the minor officials are encouraged to do their

---

[23]Reading *si* instead of *lü*.

[24]Tattooing of criminals, cutting off the nose, cutting off the feet, castration, and death.

best and the common people do not dare to be slack—these are
the duties of the prime minister. To fix rites and music, reform
conduct, spread moral education, and beautify the customs of
the people, taking cognizance of all matters and harmonizing
them into a unity—these are the duties of the high officials.[25]
To complete the Way and its virtue, establish the highest standards, unite the world in the fullest degree of order, overlook-
ing not the smallest detail, and causing all men in the world to
be obedient and submissive—these are the duties of the heavenly king. Therefore, if the affairs of government are in disorder,
it is the fault of the prime minister. If the customs of the country are faulty, it is due to the error of the high officials. And if
the world is not unified and the feudal lords are rebellious,[26]
then the heavenly king is not the right man for the job.

When[27] one has all the appurtenances of a king, he can be a
king; when he has all the appurtenances of a dictator, he can be
a dictator; when he has the appurtenances of a ruler who can
preserve his state, he will preserve his state; and when he has the
appurtenances of a ruler who will destroy his state, he will destroy it. If one heads a state of ten thousand war chariots, then
his might and authority will naturally command respect, his
fame will be widespread, and his enemies will submit. It will be
within the power of the ruler himself, not men of other states,
to regulate his safety and goodness. It will be within the power

---

[25]Following Kanaya, I take the phrase *bigong* to refer to the *sangong* or three high
officials: the grand tutor, the grand protector, and the director of music. They had
charge of affairs pertaining to manners and moral education. Some translators,
however, take *bigong* to refer to the feudal lords.

[26]Reading *bei* instead of *su* in accordance with the suggestion of Kubo Ai.

[27]The remainder of the chapter lacks Yang Liang's commentary and is difficult to
make out at numerous points. I have in general followed Kanaya and somewhat ex-
panded the original in a few places to make it intelligible in translation.

of the ruler himself, not other men, to decide whether he will
become a king or a dictator, whether he will choose preservation
or destruction. But if his might and authority are not sufficient
to intimidate his neighbors and his fame is not the kind to
spread throughout the world, then he does not yet have the
power to stand alone, so how can he hope to escape difficulties?
Threatened by the power of some evil neighbor state, he and the
rulers of other states may have to ally themselves with it and be
forced to do things they do not wish to do. But although they
may find themselves day by day imitating the deeds and actions
of the tyrant Jie, it does not necessarily mean that, given the op-
portunity, they could not become sage rulers like Yao. Only this
is not the way to win merit and fame and to assist other states
that are in danger of being wiped out. The way to win merit and
fame and to assist other states that are in danger of being wiped
out is to remain free and flourishing and to act from the sincerity of one's innermost heart. If one is truly able to administer his
state in the manner of a king, then he may become a king. If he
administers his state so as to place it in a condition of danger and
near destruction, then he will face danger and destruction.

He who is in a flourishing condition may stand upon what is
right, showing no favoritism to any side but conducting all his
affairs as he wishes; he may keep his armies at home and sit back
and watch while the evil and violent nations of the world fall
upon each other. If he regulates the teachings of his government
properly, examines carefully the rules and proposals of his officials, and encourages and educates his people, then the day will
come when his armies can stand up against the strongest forces
in the world. If he practices benevolence and righteousness,
honors the highest principles, makes his laws upright, selects
worthy and good men for his government, and looks after the
needs of his people, then the day will come when his reputation

may match in fairness that of any ruler in the world. Weighty in authority, strong in military might, fair in reputation—even the sages Yao and Shun who united the world could find nothing to add to such a ruler.

If schemers and plotters who would overthrow the state are forced to retire, then men of worth and sage wisdom will come forward of themselves. If punishments and government regulations are just, the people harmonious, and the customs of the country well moderated, then the armies will be strong, the cities secure against attack, and enemy nations will submit of their own free will. If attention is paid to agriculture, and wealth and goods are accumulated, if one does not forget to guard against lavishness and excessive expenditure, and causes the officials and common people to act in accordance with the rules and regulations, then wealth and goods will increase and the state will automatically grow rich. If these three conditions are realized, then the whole world will pay allegiance to such a ruler, and the rulers of evil states will automatically find themselves unable to use their armies against him. Why? Because no one will join them in the attack.

If they carry out a military expedition against him, it must be with the support of their own people. But if their own people favor the good ruler, look up to him as a father or mother and rejoice in him as in the fragrance of iris or orchid, and on the contrary regard their own rulers as so many wielders of branding irons and tattooing knives, as their foes and enemies, then, human nature being what it is, even if the people should be as cruel and violent as the tyrant Jie or Robber Zhi, how could they be willing to fight for the sake of men they hate and do harm to one they love? For this reason such evil rulers will be overthrown. Therefore, in ancient times there were men who began as rulers of a single state and ended by becoming rulers of the

world, but it was not because they went about making con-
quests. They conducted their government in such a way as to
make all men wish to become their subjects, and in this manner
they were able to punish the violent and suppress the wicked.
Thus when the duke of Zhou marched south, the states of the
north were resentful and asked, "Why does he neglect only us?";
and when he marched east, the states of the west grew angry and
asked, "Why does he leave us to the last?"[28] Who could stand up
against such a ruler? Therefore he who can order his state in this
way may become a true king.

He who is in a flourishing condition may hold his armies in
reserve and give his soldiers rest, may love and look after his
people, open up new lands for cultivation, fill his granaries, and
see that all necessary goods are supplied. With care he will select men of talent and promote them to office, where he will
offer rewards to encourage them and threaten strict punishments in order to restrain them from evil. He will choose men
who know how to handle such things and employ them to attend
to and manage all affairs. Then he may sit back at ease and goods
will pile up, all will be well ordered, and there will be enough of
all things to go around. When it comes to weapons and military
supplies, his war-loving enemies will day by day be smashing
and destroying theirs and leaving them strewn over the plains of
battle, while he polishes and mends his and stacks them away in
his arsenals. As for goods and grain, his enemies will day by day
be wasting theirs and pouring them out to supply the camp-
grounds, while he gathers his in and stores them in his granaries
and supply houses. As for men of talent, wise counselors, and

---

[28]Mencius (IB, II) quotes a similar passage from a lost section of the *Book of Documents* where the hero, however, is not the duke of Zhou but Tang, the founder of
the Shang dynasty.

brave and fierce warriors, his enemies will day by day be destroying and wearing theirs out in strife and battle, while he attracts more and more of them to his state, selects all those who are worthy, and trains them at his court. In this way his enemies will daily pile up depletion while he piles up abundance; they will daily pile up poverty while he piles up riches; they will daily pile up labor while he piles up ease. In the states of his enemies relations between ruler and minister, superior and inferior will be pervaded by bitterness and day by day grow more harsh and strained; while with him such relations will be marked by warmth and will daily become closer and more affectionate. Therefore he can stand by and wait for the decay of his enemies and, ordering his own state in this way, may become a dictator.

If a ruler follows ordinary customs in his behavior, attends to affairs in accordance with ordinary practice, selects ordinary men and promotes them in government, and treats his inferiors and the common people with ordinary lenience and bounty, then he may dwell in safety. If a ruler is frivolous and coarse in his behavior, hesitant and suspicious in attending to affairs, selects men for office because they flatter and are glib, and in his treatment of the common people is rapacious and grasping, then he will soon find himself in peril. If a ruler is arrogant and cruel in his behavior, attends to affairs in an irrational and perverse manner, selects and promotes men who are insidious and full of hidden schemes, and in his treatment of the common people is quick to exploit their strength and endanger their lives but slow to reward their labors and accomplishments, loves to exact taxes and duties but neglects the state of agriculture, then he will surely face destruction.

One must be careful to choose well from among these five categories, for these are the appurtenances that make one a king, a dictator, a ruler who dwells in safety, one who faces peril, or one who faces destruction. He who chooses well can control others; he who chooses badly will be controlled by others. He who chooses well may become a king; he who chooses badly will be destroyed. To be a king or to be destroyed, to control others or to be controlled by them—the two conditions are far apart indeed!

⇥ DEBATING MILITARY AFFAIRS

(Section 15)

The lord of Linwu and Xunzi were debating military affairs in the presence of King Xiaocheng of Zhao.[1] "May I ask what are the most essential points to be observed in taking up arms?" inquired the king.

The lord of Linwu replied, "Above, utilize the most seasonable times of heaven; below, take advantage of the most profitable aspects of the earth. Observe the movements of your enemy, set out after he does, but get there before him. This is the essential point in the art of using arms!"

"Not so!" objected Xunzi. "From what I have heard of the way of the ancients, the basis of all aggressive warfare and military undertaking lies in the unification of the people. If the bow and arrow are not properly adjusted, even the famous archer Yi could not hit the mark. If the six horses of the team are not properly trained, even the famous carriage driver Zaofu could not go far. If the officers and people are not devoted to

---

[1] The lord of Linwu is identified by commentators as a general of the state of Chu. Xunzi is referred to throughout the chapter as Sun Qingzi (see Introduction, p. 1). King Xiaocheng of Zhao reigned 265–245 B.C.

their leaders, even the sages Tang or Wu could not win victory. The one who is good at winning the support of his people is the one who will be good at using arms. Therefore what is really essential in military undertakings is to be good at winning the support of the people."

"I disagree," said the lord of Linwu. "In using arms, one should place the highest value upon advantageous circumstances, and should move by stealth and deception. He who is good at using arms moves suddenly and secretly, and no one knows from whence he comes. Sun Wu and Wu Qi[2] employed this method and there was no one in the world who could stand up against them. Why is it necessary to win the support of the people?"

"You do not understand," said Xunzi. "What I am speaking about are the soldiers of a benevolent man, the intentions of a true king. You speak of the value of plots and advantageous circumstances, of moving by sudden attack and stealth—but these are matters appropriate only to one of the feudal lords. Against the soldiers of a benevolent man, deceptions are of no use; they are effective only against a ruler who is rash and arrogant, whose people are worn out; they are effective only against a state in which the ruler and his subjects, superiors and inferiors, are torn apart and at odds. Therefore a tyrant like Jie may practice deception upon another Jie, and, depending upon how cleverly he proceeds, may happily achieve a certain success. But for a Jie to try to practice deception against a sage like Yao would be like trying to break a rock by throwing eggs at it, or trying to stir boiling water with your bare finger. He will be like a man consumed by fire or drowned in water.

---

[2]Two famous generals and military experts of the late 4th and 3d centuries respectively. Both are reputed authors of early works on military science, known today as the *Sunzi* and *Wuzi*.

"As for the relations between superior and inferior under the rule of a benevolent man, the various generals will be of one mind, and the three armies of the state will work together. Subjects will serve their lord and inferiors will serve their superiors like sons serving a father or younger brothers serving an elder brother. They will be like hands held up to guard the face and eyes, arms clasped to protect the breast and belly. Try to attack such a ruler by deception and you will see the hands fly up in warning and then dart forward in attack.

"Moreover, if the benevolent man rules a state which is ten *li* square, the people for a hundred *li* around will act as listeners for him; if he rules a state of a hundred *li*, a thousand *li* will listen for him; and if he rules a state of a thousand *li*, the whole region within the four seas will listen for him. He will receive clear intelligence and warning, and the whole region will draw about him in unity. Thus the soldiers of a benevolent man, when gathered together, will form themselves into companies; when spread out, they will form in ranks. In striking power they are like the long blade of the famous sword Moye; what comes beneath it will be cut off. In keenness they are like the sharp point of Moye; what falls upon it will be pierced through. Drawn up in square encampment and surrounded by sentries, they will be like a solid rock; what butts against it will be smashed, crushed, broken, defeated, and forced to fall back.[3]

"When rulers of evil and war-loving states carry out their expeditions, who can they get to accompany them? Obviously they must employ their own people. But if their own people favor the

---

[3]This last clause contains seven characters that are quite unintelligible. Commentators generally agree that they must have the meaning given in the translation, though efforts to interpret or amend the individual characters are scarcely convincing.

benevolent ruler, look up to him as to a father or mother, and rejoice in him as in the fragrance of iris or orchid, and on the contrary regard their own superiors as so many wielders of branding irons and tattooing knives, as their foes and enemies, then, human nature being what it is, even if the people should be as cruel and violent as the tyrant Jie or Robber Zhi, how could they be willing to fight for the sake of men they hate and do harm to one they love? This would be like trying to force men to do harm to their own fathers or mothers. They will surely come, therefore, and give warning to the benevolent ruler, and in that case how can the evil rulers hope to carry out their deceptions?

"Therefore, when the benevolent man rules the state, he grows day by day more illustrious. Those among the other feudal lords who lead the way in paying allegiance to him will find safety, those who lag behind will be in danger, those who oppose him on too many points will find their territory stripped away, and those who turn against him will perish. This is what the *Odes* means when it says:

> The martial king raised his banners,
> Firmly he grasped his battle-ax.
> Blazing like a fierce fire,
> Who then dared oppose us?"[4]

"Very good," replied King Xiaocheng and the lord of Linwu. "And may we ask what ways and what modes of action the true king should follow in employing his soldiers?"

Xunzi said, "Such detailed matters are of minor importance to Your Majesty, and may be left to the generals. What I would

---

[4]"Hymns of Shang," *Changfa*, Mao text no. 304. The martial king is Tang, the founder of the Shang dynasty.

like to speak about, however, are the signs which indicate whether the king and the feudal lords are strong or weak, whether they are destined to survive or to perish, and the circumstances which insure safety or invite danger.

"If the ruler is a worthy man, the state will be ordered; if he is incompetent, the state will be disordered. If he honors rites and values righteousness, the state will be ordered; if he disdains rites and despises righteousness, the state will be disordered. The ordered state will be strong, the disordered one weak. This is the basis of strength and weakness.

"If superiors have the qualities that command respect, then inferiors can be employed. If superiors do not command respect, then inferiors cannot be employed. If inferiors can be employed, the state will be strong; if not, the state will be weak. This is a constant rule of strength and weakness.

"To honor rites and seek to achieve merit is the highest manner of action. To work hard for one's stipend and value integrity is the next highest manner. To consider merit above all other things and despise integrity is the lowest manner. This is the constant principle of strength and weakness.

"He who treats his officers well will be strong; he who does not will be weak. He who loves his people will be strong; he who does not will be weak. He whose government decrees are trusted will be strong; he whose government decrees are not trusted will be weak. He whose people are unified will be strong; he whose people are not unified will be weak. He whose rewards are generous will be strong; he whose rewards are meager will be weak. He whose punishments are held in awe will be strong; he whose punishments are regarded with contempt will be weak. He whose supplies and armaments are complete and efficient will be strong; he whose supplies and armaments are crude and inefficient will be weak. He who uses his soldiers with caution will be strong; he who uses them rashly will be weak. He whose strategies proceed from a single source will be strong; he whose strategies proceed from several sources will be weak. This is the abiding rule of strength and weakness.

"The men of Qi place great emphasis upon skill in personal attack.[5] He who by such skill comes back with the head of an enemy is rewarded with eight ounces of gold levied from the men who accomplished no such deed, but outside of this there are no regular battle rewards.[6] If one is faced with an enemy who is weak and small in numbers, such methods may achieve a certain temporary success, but if the enemy is numerous and strong, one's own forces will quickly disintegrate. They will scatter like birds in flight, and it will be only a matter of days before the state will be overthrown. This method of employing soldiers will doom a state to destruction; no way leads to greater weakness. It is in fact hardly different from going to the market place and hiring day laborers to do one's fighting.

"The rulers of Wei select their foot soldiers on the basis of certain qualifications. They must be able to wear three sets of armor,[7] carry a crossbow of twelve-stone weight, bear on their backs a quiver with fifty arrows, and in addition carry a spear. They must also wear helmets on their heads, a sword at their waist, carry three days' provisions, and still be able to march a hundred *li* in one day. When men have met these qualifications, their families are exempted from *corvée* labor and are given special tax benefits on their lands and houses. Thus, although individual soldiers may grow old and their strength wane, their priv-

---

[5]Writing some 150 years later, the historian Sima Qian noted the same fact: "The people (of Qi) . . . are timid in group warfare but brave in single combat" (*Shiji* 129).
[6]Following the interpretation of Kubo Ai.
[7]Defined by commentators as breastplates, waist guards, and shin guards.

ileges cannot be readily taken away from them, and in addition it is not easy to train a sufficient number of new recruits to replace them. For this reason, though the territory of the state is large, its taxes are meager. This method of employing soldiers puts a state in grave peril.

"As for the rulers of Qin, they have only a narrow, confined area on which to settle their people. They employ them harshly, terrorize them with authority, embitter them with hardship, coax them with rewards, and cow them with punishments. They see to it that if the humbler people[8] hope to gain any benefits from their superiors, they can do so only by achieving distinction in battle. They oppress the people before employing them and make them win some distinction before granting them any benefit. Rewards increase to keep pace with achievements; thus a man who returns from battle with five enemy heads is made the master of five families in his neighborhood. In comparison with the other methods I have mentioned, this is the best one to insure a strong and populous state that will last for a long time, a wide expanse of territory that yields taxes. Therefore Qin's repeated victories during the last four generations[9] are no accident, but the result of policy.

"So the skilled attackers of Qi cannot stand up against the armed infantry of Wei, and the armed infantry of Wei cannot stand up against the fierce officers of Qin. But neither could the fierce officers of Qin come face to face with the well-regulated troops of the dictators Duke Huan of Qi or Duke Wen of Jin, nor could the troops of Duke Huan or Duke Wen possibly hold

---

[8]Omitting *tian*, which makes no sense here.
[9]Probably a reference to the reigns of Duke Xiao and Kings Hui, Wu, and Zhao of Qin, or the period from 361 to 250 B.C., when Qin was steadily growing in size and power.

out against the benevolence and righteousness of King Tang or King Wu. Before such a force they would be like something burned and shriveled, something flung against a rock.

"The soldiers of states like Qi, Wei, or Qin are all merely seeking reward or striving for some profit. They are following the ways of hired laborers or tradesmen, and as yet have not understood what it means to honor their superiors, conform to regulations, and fulfill their moral obligations. If one of the other feudal lords were truly able to imbue his people with a sense of honor, then he could rise up and menace them all without difficulty. Therefore, to attract men to military service and recruit soldiers as they do, to rely upon force and deception and teach men to covet military achievements and profit—this is the way to deceive the people. But to rely upon ritual principles and moral education—this is the way to unite them. When deception meets deception, the victory may go either way, depending upon the cleverness of the combatants. But to try to use deception to meet unity is like trying to hack down Mount Tai with an awl—no one in the world would be stupid enough no attempt it! Thus, when the true king leads forth his troops, there is no doubt of the outcome. When King Tang set out to punish Jie, and King Wu to punish Zhou, they had only to give a wave of their hands and a nod, and even the most powerful and unruly nations hastened to their service. Punishing Jie and Zhou then became no more difficult than punishing a lone commoner. This is what the 'Great Oath' means when it speaks of 'Zhou, the lone commoner.'[10]

"Those whose soldiers achieve a major degree of unity may control the world; those whose soldiers achieve only a minor degree of unity may still be strong enough to menace[11] their

---

[10]From the "Taishi" (Great Oath), a lost section of the *Book of Documents*. The section by that name in the present text is a later forgery.

[11]Reading *dai* instead of *zhi*.

enemies close by. But those who attract men to military service and recruit soldiers, rely upon deception, and teach men to covet military achievements and profit—their soldiers will sometimes win, sometimes lose, but do neither consistently. At times such men will contract their sphere of influence, at times they will expand it; at times they will survive, at times they will go under, like rivals struggling for supremacy. Military operations of this kind are like the raids of robber bands; the gentleman has nothing to do with such ways.

"Thus, for example, Tian Dan of Qi, Zhuang Qiao of Chu, Wei Yang of Qin, and Miao Ji of Yan[12] were all men who were popularly said to have been skilled in the use of soldiers. Yet, though these men achieved varying degrees of cleverness and might, they all followed essentially the same methods, and none of them ever got so far as to bring true harmony and unity to their armies. They all relied upon sudden seizures, deceptions, stratagems, and swift overthrows, and for this reason their armies were no different from robber bands. Duke Huan of Qi, Duke Wen of Jin, King Zhuang of Chu, King Helü of Wu, and King Goujian of Yue[13] were all able to attain harmony and unity in their armies,

---

[12]Tian Dan was a well-known general of Qi who, in 285–284 B.C., drove the invading troops of Yan and her allies from the state and rescued the royal house of Qi from destruction. His biography is found in *Shiji* 82. Zhuang Qiao was a general of Chu who, in the time of King Wei of Chu (339–328 B.C.), gained control of a large area west of Chu in present-day Sichuan and Guizhou provinces. He later turned against his sovereign and made himself an independent ruler in the region of Lake Dian in Yunnan. Cf. *Shiji* 116. Wei Yang, often referred to by his title Lord Shang, was the famous statesman and Legalist adviser to Duke Xiao of Qin (361–338 B.C.), whose biography is the subject of *Shiji* 68. He is the reputed author of the Legalist work, *The Book of Lord Shang*. Miao Ji is otherwise unknown.
[13]This is the usual list of the five *ba* or dictator leaders of the feudal lords. The dates of their reigns are: Duke Huan of Qi, 685–643 B.C.; Duke Wen of Jin, 636–628 B.C.; King Zhuang of Chu, 613–591 B.C.; King Helü of Wu, 514–496 B.C.; King Goujian of Yue, ?–465 B.C.

and it may therefore be said that they at least entered the realm of the true way. And yet they never grasped the essentials of the matter. So they were able to become dictators, but not to become true kings. These are the signs of strength and weakness."

"Excellent!" exclaimed King Xiaocheng and the lord of Linwu. "And now may we ask how to become a good general?"

Xunzi replied, "In knowledge, nothing is more important than discarding what is doubtful; in action, nothing is more important than avoiding mistakes; in undertakings, nothing is more important than to be without regret. Only make sure that you will not regret the undertaking, and then you need not worry about whether it will be successful or not.

"In regulations and commands, strive for strictness and authority. In rewards and punishments, strive for consistency and aptness. In establishing encampments and depots, strive to make them well-guarded and secure. In troop movements, strive for an air of gravity and deliberateness, at the same time striving for alertness and rapidity. In observing the disposition and movements of the enemy, strive to obtain the most complete and penetrating reports, and see that they are checked for reliability. In meeting the enemy in battle, proceed on the basis of what you understand thoroughly, not on the basis of what you are in doubt about. These are called the six arts.

"Do not think only of maintaining your rank as a general and shudder at the thought of losing your command. Do not press too hard for victory and forget about defeat. Do not be too stern with your own men and despise the enemy. Do not fix your eyes on gain alone and take no thought for loss. Seek ripeness in all your plans and liberality in your use of supplies. These are called the five expedients.

"There are three cases in which a general refuses to obey the command of his ruler. Though threatened with death, he cannot be made to take up a position that is untenable. Though threatened with death, he cannot be made to attack where there is no hope of victory. Though threatened with death, he cannot be made to deceive the common people. These are known as the three extremities.

"If the general, having received his commands from the ruler, relays them to the three armies, and sees to it that the three armies are properly regulated, that the officers are assigned to their proper ranks, and that all matters are correctly disposed of, then the ruler will have no particular occasion to rejoice nor the enemy to feel resentment.[14] This is called the highest type of service.

"Plan before any undertaking, and carry it out with circumspection; be as careful about the end as you are about the beginning, and end and beginning will be alike. This is the most auspicious policy. The success of all undertakings rests upon circumspection; their failure derives from negligence. Therefore, when circumspection prevails over carelessness, the result will be good fortune; when carelessness prevails over circumspection, the result will be annihilation. When planning prevails over personal desires, the result will be progress; when personal desires prevail over planning, the result will be disaster. Fight as though you were trying only to hold your ground; march as though you were already in battle; regard any success you achieve as merely lucky. Be cautious in strategy and never neglectful; be cautious in your undertakings and never neglectful; be cautious in dealings with your officers and never neglectful;

---

[14]I am not sure I understand what Xunzi means by this. Apparently he is saying that if the army is regulated according to objective principles, both the ruler and the enemy will take its efficiency as a matter of course and feel no particular emotional reaction. But perhaps the text is faulty.

be cautious in using your men and never neglectful; be cautious in regard to the enemy and never neglectful. These are called the five things that must not be neglected.

"He who carefully observes the six arts, the five expedients, and the three extremities, and who disposes of all matters with assiduity and circumspection, never allowing himself to be neglectful, may be called a true general of the world. He partakes of a godlike intelligence!"

"Very good," said the lord of Linwu. "And now may I ask about the regulations of the king's army?"

Xunzi replied, "The general dies with his drums; the carriage driver dies with the reins; the officials die at their posts; the leaders of the fighting men die in their ranks. When the army hears the sound of the drums, it advances; when it hears the sound of the bells, it retreats. Obedience to orders is counted first; achievements are counted second. To advance when there has been no order to advance is no different from retreating when there has been no order to retreat; the penalty is the same. The king's army does not kill the enemy's old men and boys; it does not destroy crops. It does not seize those who retire without a fight, but it does not forgive those who resist. It does not make prisoners of those who surrender and seek asylum. In carrying out punitive expeditions, it does not punish the common people; it punishes those who lead the common people astray. But if any of the common people fight with the enemy, they become enemies as well. Thus those who flee from the enemy forces and come in surrender shall be left to go free.[15] Kai, the prince of Wei, was enfeoffed in Song, but Cao Chulong was executed in

---

[15]Following the interpretation of Liu Shipei.

the presence of the army.[16] The Yin people who submitted to the leaders of the Zhou army, however, were allowed to live and were cared for the same as the people of Zhou. Hence, those close by sang songs and rejoiced, and those far off hastened to the Zhou leaders with the greatest speed. There was no country so remote and out of the way that it did not hurry forward to serve them and find rest and joy in their rule. All within the four seas became as one family, and wherever the report of their virtue penetrated, there was no one who did not submit. This is what is called being a true leader of the people. The *Odes* refers to this when it says:

> From west, from east,
> From south, from north,
> There were none who thought of not submitting.[17]

"A true king carries out punitive expeditions, but he does not make war. When a city is firmly guarded, he does not lay siege to it; when the soldiers resist strongly, he does not attack. When the rulers and their people of other states are happy with each other, he considers it a blessing. He does not massacre the defenders of a city; he does not move his army in secret; he does not keep his

---

[16]The prince of Wei was a brother of Zhou, the last ruler of the Yin. Having admonished Zhou in vain, he retired from court and, when King Wu attacked and overthrew Zhou, he greeted the army and acknowledged his submission. In return he was enfeoffed in Song and given the task of carrying on the sacrifices of the Yin royal family. His name is Qi, but it has here been changed by Han editors to Kai in order to avoid the taboo on the personal name of Emperor Jing of the Han. Cao Chulong is usually identified as an evil adviser to the tyrant Jie of the Xia, but Xunzi apparently takes him to be an adviser to the tyrant Zhou of the Yin.

[17]"Greater Odes," *Wenwang yousheng*, Mao text no. 244.

forces long in the field; he does not allow a campaign to last longer than one season. Therefore the people of badly ruled states delight in the report of his government; they feel uneasy under their own rulers and long for his coming."

"Excellent," said the lord of Linwu.

Chen Xiao[18] said to Xunzi, "When you talk about the use of arms, you always speak of benevolence and righteousness as being the basis of military action. A benevolent man loves others, and a righteous man acts in accordance with what is right. Why, then, would they have any recourse to arms in the first place? Those who take up arms do so only in order to contend with others and seize some spoil!"

Xunzi replied, "This is not something that you would understand. The benevolent man does indeed love others, and because he loves others, he hates to see men do them harm. The righteous man acts in accordance with what is right, and for that reason he hates to see men do wrong. He takes up arms in order to put an end to violence and to do away with harm, not in order to contend with others for spoil. Therefore, where the soldiers of the benevolent man encamp they command a godlike respect; and where they pass, they transform the people. They are like the seasonable rain in whose falling all men rejoice. Thus Yao attacked Huan Dou, Shun attacked the rulers of the Miao, Yu attacked Gong Gong, Tang attacked the ruler of the Xia, King Wen attacked Chong, and King Wu attacked Zhou. These four emperors and two kings all marched through the world with their soldiers of benevolence and righteousness. Those nearby were won by their goodness, and those far off were filled with longing by their virtue. They did not stain their swords with blood, and yet near and far alike submitted; their virtue flour-

---

[18]A disciple of Xunzi, otherwise unknown.

ished in the center and spread to the four quarters. This is what the *Odes* means when it says:

> The good man, the gentleman,
> His forms are without fault;
> His forms are without fault;
> He corrects the countries of the four quarters.[19]

Li Si[20] said to Xunzi, "For four generations now Qin has won victory. Its armies are the strongest in the world and its authority sways the other feudal lords. It did not attain this by means of benevolence and righteousness, but by taking advantage of its opportunities, that is all."

Xunzi replied, "This is not something that you would understand. When you talk about opportunities, you are speaking of opportunities that are in fact inopportune. When I speak of benevolence and righteousness, I mean opportunities that are in fact great opportunities. This benevolence and righteousness which I speak of are the means whereby government is ordered properly, and when government is properly ordered, then the people will draw close to their superiors, delight in their rulers, and think it a light matter to die for them. Therefore I have said

---

[19]"Airs of Cao," *Shijiu*, Mao text no. 152. The present *Xunzi* text quotes only the first two lines, but commentators believe that the next two lines should be added in order to make the quotation tie in with Xunzi's remarks.

[20]A native of Chu who, after studying for a time under Xunzi, traveled west to the state of Qin and gained the ear of the young king. With Li Si's advice and aid, the king in time succeeded in conquering the other states and becoming supreme ruler, taking the title of First Emperor of the Qin. Li Si, as prime minister, had much to do with the establishment of the new dynasty, but after the death of the First Emperor he was ousted from power by a court rival and in 208 B.C. was condemned to death.

that matters pertaining to the army and the leadership of the generals are of minor importance. Qin has been victorious for four generations, yet it has lived in constant terror and apprehension lest the rest of the world should someday unite and trample it down. These are the soldiers of a degenerate age, not of a nation which has grasped the true principle of leadership. Thus Tang did not have to wait until he had cornered Jie on the field of Mingtiao before he could accomplish his overthrow; King Wu did not have to wait until his victory on the day *jiazi* before he could punish Zhou for his evil deeds.[21] They had already assured victory for themselves by all their earlier deeds and actions. This is what it means to employ the soldiers of benevolence and righteousness. Now you do not try to get at the root of the matter, but look for a model in superficial appearances. This is the way to bring disorder to the world!"

Rites[22] are the highest expression of hierarchical order, the basis for strengthening the state, the way by which to create authority, the crux of achievement and fame. By proceeding in accordance with ritual, kings gain possession of the world; by ignoring it, they bring destruction to their altars of the grain and soil. Stout armor and sharp weapons are not enough to assure victory; high walls and deep moats are not enough to assure defense; stern commands and manifold penalties are not enough to assure authority. What proceeds by the way of ritual will advance; what proceeds by any other way will end in failure.

The men of Chu make armor out of sharkskin and rhinoceros hides, and it is so tough it rings like metal or stone. They carry

---

[21]The field of Mingtiao was the scene of Tang's final victory over Jie, the last ruler of the Xia; *jiazi* was the day of the sixty-day cycle upon which King Wu won final victory over Zhou, the last ruler of the Yin.

[22]The remainder of the chapter is not in anecdote form. The three paragraphs that follow are duplicated in Sima Qian's "Treatise on Rites," *Shiji* 23.

steel spears made in Yuan, sharp as the sting of a wasp, and move as nimbly and swiftly as a whirlwind. And yet Chu's troops were defeated at Qiusha and their general, Tang Mei, was killed; and from the time when Zhuang Qiao turned against the king of Chu, the state was torn apart.[23] Surely this did not come about because Chu lacked stout armor and sharp weapons. Rather it was because its leaders did not follow the proper way. They had the Ru and Ying rivers to protect them, the Yangzi and the Han as their moats; they were bounded by the forests of Deng and shielded by Mount Fangcheng. And yet the Qin forces swept down and seized the Chu capital city of Yan in Ying as easily as one might shake down a dry leaf.[24] Surely it was not because Chu lacked natural defenses and barriers to protect it. Rather it was because its leaders failed to follow the proper way. The tyrant Zhou cut out Bi Gan's heart, imprisoned Jizi, and made the punishment of the burning pillar. He murdered and massacred without season and his ministers and people were filled with terror and gave up all hope of saving their lives. Yet, when the armies of King Wu came sweeping down, none of Zhou's commands were obeyed and he found he could not rally his people about him. Surely it was not because his commands were not stern enough or his punishments not manifold. Rather it was because in leading the people he failed to follow the proper way.

In ancient times the only weapons were spears, lances, bows, and arrows, and yet enemy states did not even wait until these were used against them, but submitted at once. Men did not build walls and battlements or dig ditches and moats; they did not set up defenses and watch stations or construct war machines,

---

[23]In 300 B.C. the army of King Huai of Chu was defeated at Qiusha by the combined forces of Qin, Han, Wei and Qi. For Zhuang Qiao, see above, n. 12.

[24]Xunzi is referring to the attack against Chu led by the Qin general Bo Qi in 278 B.C., when the Qin forces seized the Chu capital and forced King Qingxiang to flee.

and yet the state was peaceful and safe, free from fear of outside aggression and secure in its position.[25] There was only one reason for this. The leaders illumined the Way and apportioned all ranks fairly; they employed the people at the proper season and sincerely loved them, so that the people moved in harmony with their superiors as shadows follow a form or echoes answer a sound. If there were any who did not follow commands, then and only then were punishments applied. Therefore, the rulers had only to punish one man and the whole world submitted. Men who had been punished bore no ill will against their superiors, for they knew that the fault lay in themselves. Therefore, the rulers seldom had to use punishments, and yet their authority was recognized by all. There was only one reason for this: they followed the proper way. In ancient times, when Yao ruled the world, he executed one man, punished two others, and after that the whole world was well ordered. This is what the old text means when it says, "let your authority inspire awe, but do not wield it; set up penalties but do not apply them."

It is the way with all men that, if they do something only for the sake of winning rewards and benefits, then, the moment they see that the undertaking may end unprofitably or in danger, they will abandon it. Therefore rewards, punishments, force, and deception are in themselves not enough to make men put forth their full efforts or risk their lives for the state. If the rulers and superiors do not treat the common people in accordance with ritual principles, loyalty, and good faith, but rely solely upon rewards, punishments, force, and deception, oppressing them and trying merely to squeeze some kind of service and achievement out of them, then when an invader comes, if entrusted with the defense of a threatened city, they will surely betray their trust; if

---

[25]Following the reading of *Shiji* 23.

led into battle against the enemy, they will invariably turn and flee; if assigned to some difficult and demanding task, they will certainly run away. The bonds that should hold them will melt, and inferiors will turn upon and seize control of their superiors. Rewards and punishments, force and deception may be the way to deal with hired laborers or tradesmen, but they are no way to unify the population of a great state or bring glory to the nation. Therefore, the men of ancient times were ashamed to resort to such ways.

Lead the people by magnifying the sound of virtue, guide them by making clear ritual principles, love them with the utmost loyalty and good faith, give them a place in the government by honoring the worthy and employing the able, and elevate them in rank by bestowing titles and rewards. Demand labor of them only at the proper season, lighten their burdens, unify them in harmony, nourish them and care for them as you would little children. Then, when the commands of government have been fixed and the customs of the people unified, if there should be those who depart from the customary ways and refuse to obey their superiors, the common people will as one man turn upon them with hatred, and regard them with loathing, like an evil force that must be exorcised. Then and only then should you think of applying penalties. Such are the kind of men who deserve severe punishment. What greater disgrace could come to them? If they try to profit by evil ways, they find themselves confronted by severe punishment. Who but a madman or a fool, perceiving such an outcome, would fail to reform?

After this the common people will become enlightened and will learn to obey the laws of their superiors, to imitate the ways of their ruler, and will find rest and delight in them. Then, if men should appear who can train themselves to do good, improve and rectify their conduct, practice ritual principles, and honor the Way, the common people will as one man show them deference and respect, will favor and praise them. Then and only then may you think of doling out rewards. Such are the kind of men who deserve lofty titles and generous emoluments. What greater glory could come to them? If they fear to suffer some loss by their virtuous ways, they find themselves supported and sustained by titles and emoluments. What man is there alive who would not wish to receive the same?

With lofty titles and generous emoluments clearly held out before him, and explicit penalties and deep disgrace unmistakably hovering behind him, though a man might have no wish to reform his ways, how could he help himself? Therefore, the people will flock about their ruler like water flowing downward. Where he is present, he commands a godlike respect; when he acts, he transforms the people (and they become obedient).[26] The violent and daring are transformed to sincerity; the prejudiced and selfish-minded are transformed to fairness; the quick-tempered and contentious are transformed to harmony. This is called the great transformation and the highest unity. The *Odes* refers to this when it says:

> The king's plans were truly sincere,
> And the country of Xu came in submission.[27]

There are three methods by which you may annex a neighboring state and bring its people under your rule: you may win them over by virtue, by force, or by wealth.

---

[26]The words in parentheses, two characters in the original, break the rhythm of the passage; either they are part of a clause the rest of which has dropped out of the text, or they do not belong here at all.

[27]"Greater Odes," *Changwu*, Mao text no. 263.

If the people of a neighboring state respect your reputation, admire your virtuous actions, and desire to become your subjects, they will throw open their gates, clear the roads, and welcome you to their cities. If you allow them to follow their old customs and remain in their old homes, the common people will all rest easy and will willingly obey your laws and commands. In this way you will acquire new territory and your power will increase; you will have added to your population and your armies will be stronger than ever. This is what it means to win over a neighbor by virtue.

If the people of a neighboring state do not respect your reputation or admire your virtuous actions, but are awed by your authority and intimidated by force, then, although they will feel no loyalty to you in their hearts, they will not dare to resist annexation. In such cases, however, you will have to enlarge your garrisons and increase your military supplies, and your government expenditures will increase likewise. In this way you will acquire new territory but your power will decrease; you will have added to your population but your armies will be weaker than before. This is what it means to win over a neighbor by force.

If the people of a neighboring state do not respect your reputation or admire your virtuous actions, but are poor and are looking for some way to get rich, are starving and in search of plenty, then they will come to you with empty bellies and gaping mouths, attracted by your food alone. In such a case, you will have to issue supplies of grain from your storehouses in order to feed them, hand out goods and wealth to enrich them, and appoint conscientious officials to look out for them, and only after three years have passed can you put faith in their loyalty. In this way you will acquire new territory but your power will decrease; you will have added to your population but the state will be poorer than before. This is what it means to win over a neighbor by wealth. Therefore I say, he who annexes a state by virtue is a true king; he who annexes it by force will be weakened; and he who annexes it by wealth will be impoverished. From ancient times to the present it has always been the same.

It is easy enough to annex territory; the difficult thing is to stabilize and maintain control over it. Qi was able to annex Song, but could not hold on to it, and so Wei snatched it away. Yan succeeded in annexing Qi, but could not hold on to it, and so Tian Dan seized control of it. Han's territory of Shangdang, a region several hundred *li* square, rich and well inhabited, chose to become part of Zhao, but Zhao could not hold on to it, and hence Qin took it away.[28] He who is able to annex territory but not to hold on to it will invariably be stripped of his acquisitions; he who can neither annex territory nor hold on to what he has will surely be destroyed. He who can hold on to territory will invariably be able to acquire more. When one can both acquire and hold on to territory, there is no limit[29] to the amount he can annex. In ancient times Tang began with the region of Bo and King Wu began with Hao, both of them areas of only a hundred *li* square. The reason they were able to unite the world under their rule and win the allegiance of all the other feudal lords was simply this: they knew how to secure their hold upon their territory.

Secure your hold on the aristocracy by means of ritual; secure your hold on the people through government. With ritual well ordered, the aristocracy will submit to your rule; with the gov-

---

[28]Qi annexed Song in 286 B.C. but lost it two years later to Wei. For Tian Dan and the invasion of Qi by Yan, see above, n. 12. The region of Shangdang, originally a part of Han, chose to become part of Zhao in 261 B.C., but three years later it was taken over by Qin.

[29]Reading *qiang* (border) instead of *jiang*.

ernment fairly administered, the people will feel safe. With the aristocracy submissive and the people content, you will attain what is called a situation of great stability. If you remain within your borders, you will be unassailable; if you march to battle, you will be strong. What you command will be done, what you forbid will cease, and the undertakings of a true king will be complete in you.

A DISCUSSION OF HEAVEN

(Section 17)

Heaven's ways are constant. It does not prevail because of a sage
like Yao; it does not cease to prevail because of a tyrant like Jie.
Respond to it with good government, and good fortune will result; respond to it with disorder, and misfortune will result. If you
encourage agriculture and are frugal in expenditures, then Heav-
en cannot make you poor. If you provide the people with the
goods they need and demand their labor only at the proper time,
then Heaven cannot afflict you with illness. If you practice the
Way and are not of two minds, then Heaven cannot bring you
misfortune. Flood or drought cannot make your people starve,
extremes of heat or cold cannot make them fall ill, and strange
and uncanny occurrences cannot cause them harm. But if you
neglect agriculture and spend lavishly, then Heaven cannot make
you rich. If you are careless in your provisions and slow to act,
then Heaven cannot make you whole. If you turn your back upon
the Way and act rashly, then Heaven cannot give you good fortune. Your people will starve even when there are no floods or
droughts; they will fall ill even before heat or cold come to oppress them; they will suffer harm even when no strange or uncanny happenings occur. The seasons will visit you as they do a

well-ordered age, but you will suffer misfortunes that a well-ordered age does not know. Yet you must not curse Heaven, for it is merely the natural result of your own actions. Therefore, he who can distinguish between the activities of Heaven and those of mankind is worthy to be called the highest type of man.

To bring to completion without acting, to obtain without seeking—this is the work of Heaven. Thus, although the sage has deep understanding, he does not attempt to exercise it upon the work of Heaven; though he has great talent, he does not attempt to apply it to the work of Heaven; though he has keen perception, he does not attempt to use it on the work of Heaven. Hence it is said that he does not compete with Heaven's work. Heaven has its seasons; earth has its riches; man has his government. Hence man may form a triad with the other two. But if he sets aside that which allows him to form a triad with the other two and longs for what they have, then he is deluded. The ranks of stars move in progression, the sun and moon shine in turn, the four seasons succeed each other in good order, the yin and yang go through their great transformations, and the wind and rain pass over the whole land. All things obtain what is congenial to them and come to life, receive what is nourishing to them and grow to completion. One does not see the process taking place, but sees only the results. Thus it is called godlike. All men understand that the process has reached completion, but none understands the formless forces that bring it about. Hence it is called the accomplishment of Heaven.[1] Only the sage does not seek to understand Heaven.

When the work of Heaven has been established and its accomplishments brought to completion, when the form of man is whole and his spirit is born, then love and hate, delight and

---

[1]Adding the word *gong* at the end of the sentence.

anger, sorrow and joy find lodging in him. These are called his heavenly emotions. Ears, eyes, nose, mouth, and body all have that which they perceive, but they cannot substitute for one another. They are called the heavenly faculties. The heart dwells in the center and governs the five faculties, and hence it is called the heavenly lord. Food and provisions are not of the same species as man, and yet they serve to nourish him and are called heavenly nourishment. He who accords with what is proper to his species will be blessed; he who turns against it will suffer misfortune. These are called the heavenly dictates. To darken the heavenly lord, disorder the heavenly faculties, reject the heavenly nourishment, defy the heavenly dictates, turn against the heavenly emotions, and thereby destroy the heavenly accomplishment is called dire disaster. The sage purifies his heavenly lord, rectifies his heavenly faculties, cherishes the heavenly nourishment, obeys the heavenly dictates, nourishes the heavenly emotions, and thereby preserves the heavenly accomplishment. In this way he understands what is to be done and what is not to be done. Hence Heaven and earth too perform their functions and all things serve him. His actions are completely ordered; his nourishment of the people is completely appropriate; his life is without injury. This is what it means to truly understand Heaven. Hence the really skilled man has things which he does not do; the really wise man has things that he does not ponder.[2]

When he turns his thoughts to Heaven, he seeks to understand only those phenomena which can be regularly expected.

---

[2]In this passage, which I fear goes rather ponderously into English, Xunzi uses the word *tian* in the sense of "Nature" or "natural." I have translated it as "Heaven" or "heavenly" throughout, however, in order to make clear the connection with what has gone before.

When he turns his thoughts to earth, he seeks to understand only those aspects that can be taken advantage of. When he turns his thoughts to the four seasons, he seeks to understand only the changes that will affect his undertakings. When he turns his thoughts to the yin and yang, he seeks to understand only the modulations which call for some action on his part. The experts may study Heaven; the ruler himself should concentrate on the Way.

Are order and disorder due to the heavens? I reply, the sun and moon, the stars and constellations revolved[3] in the same way in the time of Yu as in the time of Jie. Yu achieved order; Jie brought disorder. Hence order and disorder are not due to the heavens.

Are they then a matter of the seasons? I reply, the crops sprout and grow in spring and summer, and are harvested and stored away in autumn and winter. It was the same under both Yu and Jie. Yu achieved order; Jie brought disorder. Hence order and disorder are not a matter of the seasons.

Are they due to the land? I reply, he who acquires land may live; he who loses it will die. It was the same in the time of Yu as in the time of Jie. Yu achieved order; Jie brought disorder. Hence order and disorder are not due to the land. This is what the *Odes* means when it says:

> Heaven made a high hill;
> Tai Wang opened it up.
> He began the work
> And King Wen dwelt there in peace.[4]

---

[3]Following Kanaya, I read *huan* instead of *rui*.
[4]"Hymns of Zhou," *Tianzuo*, Mao text no. 270.

Heaven does not suspend the winter because men dislike cold; earth does not cease being wide because men dislike great distances; the gentleman does not stop acting because petty men carp and clamor. Heaven has its constant way; earth has its constant dimensions; the gentleman has his constant demeanor. The gentleman follows what is constant; the petty man reckons up his achievements. This is what the *Odes* means when it says:

> If you have no faults of conduct,
> Why be distressed at what others say?[5]

The king of Chu has a retinue of a thousand chariots, but not because he is wise. The gentleman must eat boiled greens and drink water, but not because he is stupid. These are accidents of circumstance. To be refined in purpose, rich in virtuous action, and clear in understanding; to live in the present and remember the past—these are things which are within your own power. Therefore the gentleman cherishes what is within his power and does not long for what is within the power of Heaven alone. The petty man, however, puts aside what is within his power and longs for what is within the power of Heaven. Because the gentleman cherishes what is within his power and does not long for what is within Heaven's power, he goes forward day by day. Because the petty man sets aside what is within his power and longs for what is within Heaven's power, he goes backward day by day. The same cause impels the gentleman forward day by day, and the petty man backward. What separates the two originates in this one point alone.

---

[5]No such poem is found in the present text of the *Odes*. The first line of the quotation has dropped out of the text at this point, but has been restored from the identical quotation in sec. 22.

When stars fall or trees make strange sounds,[6] all the people in the country are terrified and go about asking, "Why has this happened?" For no special reason, I reply. It is simply that, with the changes of Heaven and earth and the mutations of the yin and yang, such things once in a while occur. You may wonder at them, but you must not fear them. The sun and moon are subject to eclipses, wind and rain do not always come at the proper season, and strange stars occasionally appear. There has never been an age that was without such occurrences. If the ruler is enlightened and his government just, then there is no harm done even if they all occur at the same time. But if the ruler is benighted and his government ill-run, then it will be no benefit to him even if they never occur at all. Stars that fall, trees that give out strange sounds—such things occur once in a while with the changes of Heaven and earth and the mutations of the yin and yang. You may wonder at them, but do not fear them.

Among all such strange occurrences, the ones really to be feared are human portents. When the plowing is poorly done and the crops suffer, when the weeding is badly done and the harvest fails; when the government is evil and loses the support of the people; when the fields are neglected and the crops badly tended; when grain must be imported from abroad and sold at a high price, and the people are starving and die by the roadside— these are what I mean by human portents. When government commands are unenlightened, public works are undertaken at the wrong season, and agriculture is not properly attended to, these too are human portents. When the people are called away for *corvée* labor at the wrong season, so that cows and horses are left to breed together and the six domestic animals produce

---

[6]Xunzi is probably referring in particular to the sacred trees planted around the altar of the soil, whose rustlings and creakings were believed to have deep significance.

prodigies;[7] when ritual principles are not obeyed, family affairs and outside affairs are not properly separated, and men and women mingle wantonly, so that fathers and sons begin to doubt each other, superior and inferior become estranged, and bands of invaders enter the state—these too are human portents. Portents such as these are born from disorder, and if all three types occur at once, there will be no safety for the state. The reasons for their occurrence may be found very close at hand; the suffering they cause is great indeed. You should not only wonder at them, but fear them as well.[8]

An old text says, "Strange occurrences among the creatures of nature are not discussed in the *Documents.*" Useless distinctions, observations which are not of vital importance—these may be left aside and not tended to. But when it comes to the duties to be observed between ruler and subject, the affection between father and son, and the differences in station between husband and wife—these you must work at day after day and never neglect.

You pray for rain and it rains. Why? For no particular reason, I say. It is just as though you had not prayed for rain and it rained anyway. The sun and moon undergo an eclipse and you try to save them;[9] a drought occurs and you pray for rain; you consult the arts of divination before making a decision on some important matter. But it is not as though you could hope

---

[7]The text of the sentence up to this point appears a little farther on in the paragraph, where it makes little sense with what goes before or after. It is not certain where it belongs (nor is the meaning any too clear), but I have followed Wang Niansun's suggestion in inserting it here.

[8]Reading *yi* instead of *bu.*

[9]According to *Zuozhuan*, Duke Wen 15th year, when an eclipse occurs, the king should beat a drum at the altar of the soil and the feudal lords should beat drums in their courts in order to drive it away.

to accomplish anything by such ceremonies. They are done merely for ornament. Hence the gentleman regards them as ornaments, but the common people regard them as supernatural. He who considers them ornaments is fortunate; he who considers them supernatural is unfortunate.

In the heavens nothing is brighter than the sun and moon; on earth nothing is brighter than fire and water; among natural objects nothing is brighter than pearls and jewels; among men nothing is brighter than ritual principles. If the sun and moon did not rise high in the sky, their splendor would not be seen; if fire and water did not accumulate into a mass, their glow and moisture would not spread abroad; if pearls and jewels did not come to light, then kings and lords would not prize them. So if ritual principles are not applied in the state, then its fame and accomplishment will not become known. The fate of man lies with Heaven; the fate of the nation lies in ritual. If the ruler of men honors rites and promotes worthy men, he may become a true king. If he relies upon laws and loves the people, he may become a dictator. If he cares only for profit and engages in much deceit, he will be in danger. And if he engrosses himself in plots and schemes, subversion and secret evil, he will be destroyed.

Is it better to exalt Heaven and think of it,
Or to nourish its creatures and regulate them?
Is it better to obey Heaven and sing hymns to it,
Or to grasp the mandate of Heaven and make use of it?
Is it better to long for the seasons and wait for them,
Or to respond to the seasons and exploit them?
Is it better to wait for things to increase of themselves,
Or to apply your talents and transform them?
Is it better to think of things but regard them as outside you,

Or to control things and not let them slip your grasp?
Is it better to long for the source from which things are born,
Or to possess the means to bring them to completion?[10]

Hence if you set aside what belongs to man and long for what belongs to Heaven, you mistake the nature of all things.

What the hundred kings of antiquity never departed from— this may serve as the abiding principle of the Way. To the ups and downs of history, respond with this single principle. If you apply it well, there will be no disorder; but if you do not understand it, you will not know how to respond to change. The essence of this principle has never ceased to exist. Disorder is born from misunderstanding of it; order consists in applying it thoroughly. If you harmonize with what is best in the Way, all will go well; if you distort what is best in the Way, you cannot govern effectively; if you mistake what is best in the Way, you will be led into grave error.

When men wade across a river, they mark the deep places; but if the markers are not clear, those who come after will fall in. He who governs the people marks the Way; but if the markers are not clear, disorder will result. Rites are the markers. He who does away with rites blinds the world; and when the world is blinded, great disorder results. Hence, if the Way is made clear in all its parts, different marks set up to indicate the outside and inside, and the dark and light places are made constant, then the pits which entrap the people can be avoided.

The ten thousand beings are only one corner of the Way. One species of being is only one corner of the ten thousand beings. The stupid man is only one corner of one species. He himself believes that he understands the Way, though of course he

---

[10]This section is rhymed.

does not. Shenzi[11] could see the advantages of holding back, but not the advantages of taking the lead. Laozi could see the advantages of humbling oneself, but not the advantages of raising one's station. Mozi could see the advantages of uniformity, but not those of diversity. Songzi[12] could see the advantages of having few desires, but not those of having many. If everyone holds back and no one takes the lead, then there will be no gate to advancement for the people. If everyone humbles himself and no one tries to improve his station, then the distinctions between eminent and humble will become meaningless. If there is only uniformity and no diversity, then the commands of government can never be carried out. If there is only a lessening of desires and never an increase, then there will be no way to educate and transform the people.[13] This is what the *Documents* means when it says: "Do not go by what you like, but follow the way of the king; do not go by what you hate, but follow the king's road."[14]

---

[11]Shen Dao, a Daoist-Legalist thinker who, according to the "Tianxia" chapter of *Zhuangzi*, preached a doctrine of passivity.

[12]Song Jian, a philosopher who, according to the same source, taught a life of frugality and few desires.

[13]Because they will not be attracted by the hope of reward.

[14]From the "Hongfan" (Great Plan).

A DISCUSSION OF RITES

(Section 19)

What is the origin of ritual? I reply: man is born with desires. If his desires are not satisfied for him, he cannot but seek some means to satisfy them himself. If there are no limits and degrees to his seeking, then he will inevitably fall to wrangling with other men. From wrangling comes disorder and from disorder comes exhaustion. The ancient kings hated such disorder, and therefore they established ritual principles in order to curb it, to train men's desires and to provide for their satisfaction. They saw to it that desires did not overextend the means for their satisfaction, and material goods did not fall short of what was desired. Thus both desires and goods were looked after and satisfied. This is the origin of rites.

Rites are a means of satisfaction. Grain-fed and grass-fed animals, millet and wheat, properly blended with the five flavors—these are what satisfy the mouth. The odors of pepper, orchid, and other sweet-smelling plants—these are what satisfy the nose. The beauties of carving and inlay, embroidery and pattern—these are what satisfy the eye. Bells and drums, strings and woodwinds—these are what satisfy the ear. Spacious rooms and secluded halls, soft mats, couches, benches, armrests and cushions—these are what satisfy the body. Therefore I say that rites are a means of providing satisfaction.

The gentleman, having provided a means for the satisfaction of desires, is also careful about the distinctions to be observed. What do I mean by distinctions? Eminent and humble have their respective stations, elder and younger their degrees, and rich and poor, important and unimportant, their different places in society. Thus the Son of Heaven has his great carriage spread with soft mats to satisfy his body. By his side are placed fragrant herbs to satisfy his nose, and before him the carved carriage decorations to satisfy his eye. The sound of carriage bells and the Wu and Xiang music when he is proceeding slowly, the Shao and Hu music when he is proceeding rapidly, give satisfaction to his ear. Nine dragon banners fly to satisfy his desire for a symbol of trust. Paintings of a recumbent rhinoceros and a solitary tiger, horse girths of water-dragon pattern, fine woven spreads, and dragon-head ornaments satisfy his desire for awesome spectacle. And the horses which draw his great carriage must be of the utmost reliability[1] and highly trained before he will consent to ride. In this way he satisfies his desire for safety.

[As for the king's officials] let them understand clearly that to advance in the face of death and to value honor is the way to satisfy their desire for life; to spend and to supply what goods are needed is the way to satisfy their desire for wealth; to conduct themselves with respect and humility is the way to satisfy their desire for safety; and to obey ritual principles and good order in all things is the way to satisfy their emotions. He who seeks only to preserve his life at all cost will surely suffer death. He who strives only for profit at all cost will surely suffer loss. He who thinks that safety lies in indolence and idleness alone will surely

[1]Reading *xin* instead of *bei* in accordance with the parallel text in *Shiji* 23.

face danger. He who thinks that happiness lies only in gratifying the emotions will surely face destruction.

Therefore, if a man concentrates upon fulfilling ritual principles, then he may satisfy both his human desires and the demands of ritual; but if he concentrates only upon fulfilling his desires, then he will end by satisfying neither. The Confucians make it possible for a man to satisfy both; the Mohists cause him to satisfy neither. This is the difference between the Confucians and the Mohists.

Rites have three bases. Heaven and earth are the basis of life, the ancestors are the basis of the family, and rulers and teachers are the basis of order. If there were no Heaven and earth, how could man be born? If there were no ancestors, how would the family come into being? If there were no rulers and teachers, how would order be brought about? If even one of these were lacking, there would be no safety for man. Therefore rites serve Heaven above and earth below, honor the ancestors, and exalt rulers and teachers. These are the three bases of rites.

The king honors the founder of his family as an equal of Heaven, the feudal lords would not dare to dismantle the mortuary temples of their ancestors, and the high ministers and officials maintain constant family sacrifices. In this way they distinguish and pay honor to the beginners of their family. To honor the beginning is the basis of virtue.

The Son of Heaven alone performs the suburban sacrifice to Heaven; altars of the soil may not be established by anyone lower than a feudal lord; but sacrifices such as the *tan* may be carried out by the officials and high ministers as well.[2] In this way rites distinguish and make clear that the exalted should

---

[2]Reading *tan* instead of *dao* and translating in accordance with the interpretation of Liu Shipei. But the passage is far from clear.

serve the exalted and the humble serve the humble, that great corresponds to great and small to small.

He who rules the world sacrifices to seven[3] generations of ancestors; he who rules a state sacrifices to five generations; he who rules a territory of five chariots[4] sacrifices to three generations; he who rules a territory of three chariots sacrifices to two generations.[5] He who eats by the labor of his hands is not permitted to set up an ancestral temple. In this way the rites distinguish and make clear that the merit accumulated by the ancestors over the generations is great. Where the merit is great, it will dispense widespread blessing; where the merit is meager, the blessing will be limited.

In the triennial great sacrificial feast, one places the water goblet in the highest place, lays out raw fish on the offering table, and offers unflavored soup, thus showing honor to the unadorned basis of food and drink. At the seasonal sacrificial feast, one places the water goblet in the highest place but fills it with wine and sweet spirits; one offers first glutinous and nonglutinous millet, and then gives the spirit representative[6] rice and common millet; while at the monthly sacrifice, one proffers first the plain soup, and then gives the spirit representative his fill of all kinds of delicacies. These last two ceremonies honor the basis

---

[3]Reading "seven" instead of "ten" in accordance with the parallel passages in *Shiji* 23, *Dadai liji* 1, and *Guliang zhuan*, Duke Xi 15th year.

[4]In early times an area 10 *li* square was said to have made up a unit called a *cheng* which was responsible for supplying one war chariot. Hence this is a territory 50 *li* square.

[5]As is made clear in the *Guliang* passage cited in n. 3 above, these four categories correspond to the four large divisions of the aristocracy: the Son of Heaven, the feudal lords, the high ministers (*dafu*), and the officials or men of breeding (*shi*).

[6]The impersonator of the dead who sits at the sacrificial feast and eats the food on behalf of the ancestors.

and at the same time bring men close to the practical uses of food. To honor the basis is called good order; to become familiar with practical usage is called good reason. When these two aspects have been combined and completed with the proper forms, and all finds rest in a single unifying principle—this is called the highest flourishing of rites.

Hence, the placing of the goblet filled with water in the highest place, the laying out of raw fish on the offering table, the presentation of the unflavored soup—all these acts have the same significance [i.e., they indicate respect for the basic materials of the meal]. The fact that the impersonator of the spirits does not finish the cup of wine handed to him by the server, that at the completion of the mourning rites he does not taste the food laid out on the offering table, that after receiving food from the three servers, he takes no more to eat—all these have the same meaning [i.e., that the ceremonies are completed]. In the wedding ceremony, before the father of the groom has given the groom a cup of wine and sent him to fetch the bride; in the sacrifice at the ancestral temple, when the impersonator of the dead has not yet entered the hall; when someone has just died and the corpse has not yet been dressed—all these are similar moments [i.e., moments before the ceremonies proper begin]. The spreading of a plain white cloth in the imperial carriage, the donning of the hempen cap at the suburban sacrifice, and the wearing of an only partly tied hempen sash during the mourning rites—all these have the same significance [i.e., they are symbols of unadorned simplicity]. And it is for the same reason that, at the three-years' mourning for a parent, the lamentation is without rhythm or fixed pattern; and, at the singing of the Pure Temple song,[7] only one man sings and

[7]One of the "Hymns of Zhou" in the *Book of Odes*, Mao text no. 266.

three harmonize with him, only one bell is played, with the leather rattle above it, and the zithers have red strings and holes in the bottom to give them a dull tone.[8]

All rites begin in simplicity, are brought to fulfillment in elegant form, and end in joy. When rites are performed in the highest manner, then both the emotions and the forms embodying them are fully realized; in the next best manner, the emotional content and the forms prevail by turns; in the poorest manner, everything reverts to emotion and finds unity in that alone.

Through rites Heaven and earth join in harmony, the sun and moon shine, the four seasons proceed in order, the stars and constellations march, the rivers flow, and all things flourish; men's likes and dislikes are regulated and their joys and hates made appropriate. Those below are obedient, those above are enlightened; all things change but do not become disordered; only he who turns his back upon rites will be destroyed. Are they not wonderful indeed? When they are properly established and brought to the peak of perfection, no one in the world can add to or detract from them. Through them the root and the branch are put in proper order; beginning and end are justified; the most elegant forms embody all distinctions; the most penetrating insight explains all things. In the world those who obey the dictates of ritual will achieve order; those who turn against them will suffer disorder. Those who obey them will win safety; those who turn against them will court danger. Those who obey them will be preserved; those who turn against them will be lost. This is something that the petty man cannot comprehend.

The meaning of ritual is deep indeed. He who tries to enter it with the kind of perception that distinguishes hard and white,

---

[8]This paragraph is a mass of technical terms, many of them of doubtful meaning. I have followed Kanaya's emendations and interpretation throughout.

same and different, will drown there.[9] The meaning of ritual is
great indeed. He who tries to enter it with the uncouth and
inane theories of the system-makers will perish there. The
meaning of ritual is lofty indeed. He who tries to enter with the
violent and arrogant ways of those who despise common customs and consider themselves to be above other men will meet
his downfall there.

If the plumb line is properly stretched, then there can be no
doubt about crooked and straight; if the scales are properly
hung, there can be no doubt about heavy and light; if the T
square and compass are properly adjusted, there can be no doubt
about square and round; and if the gentleman is well versed in
ritual, then he cannot be fooled by deceit and artifice. The line
is the acme of straightness, the scale is the acme of fairness, the
T square and compass are the acme of squareness and round-
ness, and rites are the highest achievement of the Way of man.
Therefore, those who do not follow and find satisfaction in rites
may be called people without direction, but those who do follow
and find satisfaction in them are called men of direction.

He who dwells in ritual and can ponder it well may be said to
know how to think; he who dwells in ritual and does not change
his ways may be said to be steadfast. He who knows how to think
and to be steadfast, and in addition has a true love for ritual—he
is a sage. Heaven is the acme of loftiness, earth the acme of
depth, the boundless the acme of breadth, and the sage the acme
of the Way. Therefore the scholar studies how to become a
sage; he does not study merely to become one of the people
without direction.

Ritual uses material goods for its performance, follows the distinctions of eminent and humble in creating its forms, varies its

---

[9]A reference to the Logicians.

quantities in accordance with differences of station, and varies its degree of lavishness in accordance with what is appropriate. When form and meaning are emphasized and emotional content and practical use slighted, rites are in their most florid state. When form and meaning are slighted and emphasis placed upon emotion and practical use, rites are in their leanest state. When form and meaning, and emotion and practical use, are treated as the inside and outside or the front and back of a single reality and are both looked after, then rites have reached the middle state. Therefore the gentleman understands how to make rites florid and how to make them lean, but he chooses to abide in the middle state, and no matter whether he walks or runs, hurries or hastens, he never abandons it. It is his constant world and dwelling. He who abides in it is a gentleman and a man of breeding; he who abandons it is a commoner. He who dwells in it, who wanders widely and masters all its corners and gradations, is a sage. His bounty is the accumulation of ritual; his greatness is the breadth of ritual; his loftiness is the flourishing of ritual; his enlightenment is the mastery of ritual. This is what the *Odes* means when it says:

> Their rites and ceremonies are entirely according to rule,
> Their laughter and talk are entirely appropriate.[10]

Rites are strictest in their ordering of birth and death. Birth is the beginning of man, death his end. When both beginning and end are good, man's way is complete. Therefore the gentleman is reverent in his treatment of the beginning and careful in his treatment of the end, regarding both with the same gravity. This is the way of the gentleman and the highest flowering of

---

[10]"Lesser Odes," *Chuci*, Mao text no. 209.

ritual principle. To be generous in the treatment of the living but skimpy in the treatment of the dead is to show reverence for a being who has consciousness and contempt for one who has lost it. This is the way of an evil man and an offense against the heart. The gentleman would be ashamed to treat even a lowly slave in a way that offends the heart; how much more ashamed would he be to treat those whom he honors and loves in such a way! The rites of the dead can be performed only once for each individual, and never again. They are the last occasion upon which the subject may fully express respect for his ruler, the son express respect for his parents.

To fail to treat the living with sincere generosity and reverent formality is the way of a rustic; to fail to bury the dead with sincere generosity and reverent formality is the way of a miser. The gentleman despises rusticity and is ashamed of miserliness. Hence the inner and outer coffins of the Son of Heaven consist of seven[11] layers; those of the feudal lords consist of five layers; those of the high ministers, three layers; and those of the officials, two layers. In addition, there are various rules governing the amount and quality of grave clothes and food offerings for each rank, and the type of coffin decorations and ornaments appropriate for each station, whereby reverence is expressed in outward form. In this way life and death, beginning and end, are treated the same and men's longings are satisfied. This is the way of the former kings and the highest expression of the duty of a loyal subject and a filial son.

At the funeral of the Son of Heaven, notification is sent throughout the area within the four seas and the feudal lords are called together. At the funeral of one of the feudal lords, notification is sent to allied states and their high ministers are called

---

[11]Reading "seven" instead of "ten."

together. At the funeral of a high minister, notification is sent throughout his own state and the eminent officials are called together. At the funeral of an official, notification is sent throughout his district and his friends are called together. At the funeral of a commoner, his family and close neighbors are gathered together and notification is sent throughout his community. At the funeral of an executed criminal, however, his family and neighbors do not gather together, but only his wife and children. His inner and outer coffin is only three inches thick, with only three sets of grave clothes, and no decorations for the coffin. The funeral procession may not venture out by day, but must go in the evening, as though to bury someone who has died by the roadside, and the members of the family wear ordinary clothes when they go to the burial. On returning from the burial, they perform no ritual lamentations, wear no mourning garments, and observe none of the mourning periods commonly observed for near or distant kin, but each returns to his regular activities and goes about his business as before. To bury a person in this way and fail to conduct any mourning for him indicates the highest degree of disgrace.[12]

Rites are strictest in dealing with auspicious and inauspicious occasions, making certain that they do not impinge upon each other. When the silk floss is held up to the dead man's nose to make certain that he is no longer breathing, then the loyal subject or the filial son realizes that his lord or parent is very sick indeed, and yet he cannot bring himself to order the articles needed for the laying in the coffin or the dressing of the corpse. Weeping and trembling, he still cannot stop hoping that the

---

[12]Xunzi's description of the burial of the disgraced criminal closely parallels what Mozi advocated as the burial practices of the ancient kings and the ideal for all men. See *Mozi*, sec. 25, "Moderation in Funerals: Part III."

dead will somehow come back to life; he has not yet ceased to treat the dead man as living. Only when he has resigned himself to the fact that the person is really dead can he go about making preparations for the funeral. Therefore, even in the best appointed household, two days will elapse before the dead can be laid in the coffin, and three days before the family will don mourning clothes. Only then will notification of the death be sent out to those far away, and those in charge of the funeral begin to gather the necessary articles. The period during which the dead lies in state in the coffin should not exceed seventy days, nor be less than fifty. Why? Because in this period of time those who must come from distant places will have time to arrive, all necessary articles can be procured, and all affairs attended to. This is the way of greatest loyalty, the height of propriety, and the finest of forms. After this, divination shall be made in the morning[13] to determine the day of burial, and in the evening to determine the place of burial, and then the burial shall be conducted. At such a time, what man could bear to do what duty forbids, or could fail to carry out what duty demands? Hence the three months of preparation for burial symbolizes that one wishes to provide for the dead as one would for the living, and to give the dead the proper accoutrements. It is not that one detains the dead and keeps him from his grave simply in order to satisfy the longings of the living. It is a token of the highest honor and thoughtfulness.

It is the custom in all mourning rites to keep changing and adorning the appearance of the dead person, to keep moving him farther and farther away, and as time passes, to return gradually to one's regular way of life. It is the way with the dead that, if they are not adorned, they become ugly, and if they become

---

[13]Reading *rizhao* instead of *yuezhao*, in accordance with the suggestion of Liu Shipei.

ugly, then one will feel no grief for them. Similarly, if they are kept too close by, one becomes contemptuous of their presence; when one becomes contemptuous of them, one begins to loathe them, and if one begins to loathe them, one will grow careless[14] of them and cease to treat them with reverence. If suddenly a man's honored parent dies, and yet in burying him he fails to show either grief or reverence, then he is no better than a beast. The gentleman is ashamed to have such a thing happen, and therefore he adorns the dead in order to disguise their ugliness, moves them gradually farther away in order to maintain the proper reverence, and in time returns to his regular way of life in order to look after the wants of the living.

Rites trim what is too long and stretch out what is too short, eliminate surplus and repair deficiency, extend the forms of love and reverence, and step by step bring to fulfillment the beauties of proper conduct. Beauty and ugliness, music and weeping, joy and sorrow are opposites, and yet rites make use of them all, bringing forth and employing each in its turn. Beauty, music, and joy serve to induce an attitude of tranquility and are employed on auspicious occasions. Ugliness, weeping, and sorrow induce an attitude of inquietude and are employed on inauspicious occasions. But though beauty is utilized, it should never reach the point of sensuousness or seductiveness, and though ugliness is utilized, it should never go as far as starvation or self-injury. Though music and joy are utilized, they should never become lascivious and abandoned, and though weeping and sorrow are utilized, they should never become frantic or injurious to health. If this is done, then rites have achieved the middle state.

Changes of feeling and manner should be sufficient to indicate whether the occasion is an auspicious or an inauspicious

---

[14]Reading *dai* instead of *wang* in accordance with the suggestion of Kubo Ai.

one, and to exemplify the proper degree of eminence or humbleness, of nearness or distance of kinship, but that is all. Anything that goes beyond this is wrong, and no matter how difficult it may be to perform, the gentleman will despise it. Thus, in a period of mourning, for the mourner to measure the quantity of his food before eating, to measure the size of his waist before tying his sash, and to strive deliberately for a distraught and emaciated appearance is the way of evil men. It does not represent the proper form of ritual principle nor the proper emotions of a filial son, but is done only for the sake of effect.

Smiles and a beaming face, sorrow and a downcast look—these are expressions of the emotions of joy or sorrow which come with auspicious or inauspicious occasions, and they appear naturally in the countenance. Songs and laughter, weeping and lamentation—these too are expressions of the emotions of joy or sorrow which come with auspicious or inauspicious occasions, and they appear naturally in the sound of the voice. The partaking of grass-fed and grain-fed animals, rice and millet, wine and sweet spirits, fish and meat, as well as of thick and thin gruel, beans and bean sprouts, water and water in which rice has been washed—these are expressions of the emotions of joy or sorrow which come with auspicious or inauspicious occasions, and are expressed naturally in one's food and drink. The wearing of ceremonial caps, embroidered robes, and patterned silks, or of fasting clothes and mourning clothes and sashes, straw sandals, and hempen robes—these are expressions of the emotions of joy or sorrow which come with auspicious or inauspicious occasions, and are expressed naturally in one's manner of dress. The use of spacious rooms and secluded halls, soft mats, couches and benches, armrests and cushions, or of huts of thatch and lean-tos, mats of twig and pillows of earth—these are expressions of the emotions of joy or sorrow which come with

auspicious or inauspicious occasions, and are expressed naturally in one's choice of a dwelling.[15]

The beginnings of these two emotions are present in man
from the first. If he can trim or stretch them, broaden or narrow
them, add to or take from them, express them completely and
properly, fully and beautifully, seeing to it that root and branch,
beginning and end are in their proper place, so that he may serve
as a model to ten thousand generations, then he has achieved
true ritual. But only a gentleman of thorough moral training and
practice is capable of understanding how to do this.

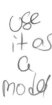

[Therefore[16] it is said that human nature is the basis and raw
material, and conscious activity is responsible for what is
adorned, ordered, and flourishing. If there were no human nature, there would be nothing for conscious activity to work
upon, and if there were no conscious activity, then human nature would have no way to beautify itself. Only when nature and
conscious activity combine does a true sage emerge and perform
the task of unifying the world. Hence it is said that when Heav-
en and earth combine, all things are born, when the yin and
yang act upon each other, all changes are produced, and when
nature and conscious activity join together, the world is well ordered. Heaven can give birth to creatures but it cannot order
them; earth can bear man up but it cannot govern him. All creatures of the universe, all who belong to the species of man, must

---

[15]In translating the numerous technical terms in this passage, I have followed
Kanaya throughout.

[16]This paragraph seems to have little to do with what goes before or after and almost certainly does not belong here. In wording and thought it is most closely allied to sec. 23, "Man's Nature Is Evil." Probably five or six of the bamboo slips
upon which the text of that section was originally written dropped out and were
mistakenly inserted here.

await the sage before they can attain their proper places. This is what the *Odes* means when it says:

> He cherishes and mollifies all the spirits,
> Even those of the River and the High Mountain.[17]]

In the funeral rites, one adorns the dead as though they were still living, and sends them to the grave with forms symbolic of life. They are treated as though dead, and yet as though still alive, as though gone, and yet as though still present. Beginning and end are thereby unified.

When a person has died, one first of all washes the hair and body, arranges them properly, and places food in the mouth, symbolizing that one treats the dead as though living. (If the hair is not washed, it is combed with a wet comb in three strokes; if the body is not bathed, it is wiped with a wet cloth in three strokes). The ears are closed with wads of silk floss, raw rice is placed in the mouth, and the mouth is stopped with a dried cowry shell. These are acts which are the opposite of what one would do for a living person. One dresses the corpse in underwear and three layers of outer garments and inserts the tablet of office in the sash, but adds no sash buckle; one adds a face cover and eye shield and arranges the hair, but does not put on any hat or hat pin. One writes the name of the deceased on a piece of cloth and fixes it to a wooden tablet, so that the coffin will not be lacking a name. As for the articles placed in the coffin, the hats have bands but no strings to tie them to the head; the jars and wine flagons are empty and have nothing in them; there are mats but no couches or armrests. The carving on the wooden articles

---

[17]"Hymns of Zhou," *Shimai*, Mao text no. 273.

and the moulding of the pottery are left unfinished, the rush and bamboo articles are such as cannot be used; the reeds and pipes are complete but cannot be sounded; the lutes and zithers are strung but not tuned. A carriage is buried with the coffin but the horses are taken back home, indicating that the carriage will not be used.

Articles that had belonged to the dead when he was living are gathered together and taken to the grave with him, symbolizing that he has changed his dwelling. But only token articles are taken, not all that he used, and though they have their regular shape, they are rendered unusable. A carriage is driven to the grave and buried there, but it has no bells or leather fixtures, no bit or reins attached. All this is done to make clear that these things will not actually be used. The dead man is treated as though he had merely changed his dwelling, and yet it is made clear that he will never use these things. This is all done in order to emphasize the feelings of grief. Thus the articles used by the dead when he was living retain the form but not the function of the common article, and the spirit articles prepared especially for the dead man have the shape of real objects but cannot be used.

It is true of all rites that, when they deal with the living, their purpose is to ornament joy, when they deal with the dead, to ornament grief, when they pertain to sacrifices, to ornament reverence, and when they pertain to military affairs, to ornament majesty. This is true of the rites of all kings, an unchanging principle of antiquity and the present, though I do not know when the custom began.

The grave and grave mound in form imitate a house; the inner and outer coffin in form imitate the sideboards, top, and front and back boards of a carriage; the coffin covers and decorations and the cover of the funeral carriage in form imitate the curtains and hangings of a door or room; the wooden lining and framework of the grave pit in form imitate railings and roof. The funeral rites have no other purpose than this: to make clear the principle of life and death, to send the dead man away with grief and reverence, and to lay him at last in the ground. At the interment one reverently lays his form away; at the sacrifices one reverently serves his spirit; and by means of inscriptions, eulogies, and genealogical records one reverently hands down his name to posterity. In serving the living, one ornaments the beginning; in sending off the dead, one ornaments the end. When beginning and end are fully attended to, then the duties of a filial son are complete and the way of the sage has reached its fulfillment. To deprive the dead for the sake of the living is niggardly; to deprive the living for the sake of the dead is delusion; and to kill the living and force them to accompany the dead is hideous. To bury the dead in the same general manner that one would send off the living, but to make certain that both living and dead, beginning and end are attended to in the most appropriate and fitting fashion—this is the rule of ritual principle and the teaching of the Confucian school.

What is the purpose of the three-year mourning period? I reply: it is a form which has been set up after consideration of the emotions involved; it is an adornment to the group and a means of distinguishing the duties owed to near or distant relatives, eminent or humble. It can neither be lengthened nor shortened. It is a method that can neither be circumvented nor changed. When a wound is deep, it takes many days to heal; where there is great pain, the recovery is slow. I have said that the three-year mourning period is a form set up after consideration of the emotions involved, because at such a time the pain of grief is most intense. The mourning garments and the cane of the mourner, the hut where he lives, the gruel he eats, the twig mat and pillow of earth he sleeps on—these are the adornments of the intense pain of his grief.

The three-year mourning period comes to an end with the twenty-fifth month. At that time the grief and pain have not yet come to an end, and one still thinks of the dead with longing, but ritual decrees that the mourning shall end at this point. Is it not because the attendance on the dead must sometime come to an end, and the moment has arrived to return to one's daily life?

All living creatures between heaven and earth which have blood and breath must possess consciousness, and nothing that possesses consciousness fails to love its own kind. If any of the animals or great birds happens to become separated from the herd or flock, though a month or a season may pass, it will invariably return to its old haunts, and when it passes its former home it will look about and cry, hesitate and drag its feet before it can bear to pass on. Even among tiny creatures the swallows and sparrows will cry with sorrow for a little while before they fly on. Among creatures of blood and breath, none has greater understanding than man; therefore man ought to love his parents until the day he dies.

Should we set our standard by the way of stupid and evil-minded men? But they have forgotten by evening the parent who died this morning, and if we are to permit such ways, then we will become worse than the very birds and beasts. How could we live in the same community with such men and hope to escape disorder? Should we then set our standard by the way of cultured and morally trained gentlemen? But to them the twenty-five months of the three-year mourning period pass as swiftly as a running horse glimpsed through a crack in the wall. If we adopt their ways, the mourning period will never come to an end. Therefore the former kings and sages adopted a middle position in fixing their standard. They allowed time for all proper forms and reasonable duties to be carried out, and decreed that the mourning period should then end.

How is the mourning period divided up? For parents it is divided on the basis of the year.[18] Why? Because in that time heaven and earth have completed their changes, the four seasons have run their course, and all things in the universe have made a new beginning. The former kings noted this and took it as a model. Why then does mourning extend into the third year? The former kings wished to increase the honor paid, and therefore they doubled the period and made it two years. Why do the mourning periods for some relatives last for only nine months or less? In order to show that they do not reach the completion of a year. Thus the three-year period expresses the highest degree of honor, while the three-month period of coarse garments or the five-month period of *xiaogong* garments expresses the lowest degree, and the year and the nine-month mourning periods fall in between. The former kings looked up and took their model from heaven, looked down and took their model from the earth, looked about and took their rules from mankind. Such rules represent the ultimate principle of community harmony and unity. Therefore, the three-year mourning period is the highest expression of the way of man and the mark of greatest honor, a custom followed by all the kings, an unchanging principle for ancient times and the present.[19]

----

[18]According to the description of mourning rites in *Liji* 37, a memorial sacrifice called *xiaoxiang* was performed at the end of one year of mourning, and a second called *daxiang* at the end of two years. Xunzi considers that the mourning period comes to an end with the second, i.e., in the 25th month, though other early texts treat it as ending in the 27th month, when the so-called *tan* sacrifice is performed.
[19]Recently found archeological evidence indicates, however, that the three-year mourning period was not a custom of early Zhou times, but probably originated around the time of Confucius. The text of this passage on the three-year mourning period has been copied into the *Liji* or *Book of Rites* and comprises nearly all of sec. 38.

Why does the mourning for a ruler last for three years? The ruler is the lord of order and good government, the font of form and reason, the model of feeling and manner. If all men join together and pay him the highest honor, is this not fitting? The *Odes* says:

> Just and gentle is the true prince,
> Father and mother to his people.[20]

This indicates that men have always looked up to their ruler as to a father or a mother. A father can beget a child, but he cannot suckle it. A mother can suckle it, but she cannot instruct and educate it. The ruler can not only feed his people, but can also educate them wisely. Is three years not in fact too short a time to mourn for him? One mourns three months for the wet nurse who suckled one, and nine months for the nursemaid who clothed one, yet the ruler does far more than this for his people. Is three years not in fact too short a time to mourn for him? With him there is order; without him there is chaos; for he is the arbiter of proper form. With him there is safety; without him there is danger; for he is the arbiter of proper feeling. Since these two faculties combine in him, three years is in fact too short a period to mourn for him, though it would be impractical to try to extend the period further.

What is the purpose of the three months of lying in state? It is to give gravity and importance to the occasion, to express honor and affection, before one finally moves the dead one, escorts him from his house, and takes him to his final resting place in the grave mound. The former kings were afraid that the process would lack a fitting form, and therefore they calculated

---

[20]"Greater Odes," *Jiongzhuo*, Mao text no. 251.

the proper time needed and allowed a sufficient number of days. Thus, for the Son of Heaven the period is seven months, for the feudal lords, five months, and for the high ministers and others, three months. In this way sufficient time is allowed for all necessary matters to be attended to and completed, for all forms to be carried out and all articles needed for the burial to be supplied. To allow such a period of time is in accordance with the Way.

The sacrificial rites originate in the emotions of remembrance and longing for the dead. Everyone is at times visited by sudden feelings of depression and melancholy longing. A loyal minister who has lost his lord or a filial son who has lost a parent, even when he is enjoying himself among congenial company, will be overcome by such feelings. If they come to him and he is greatly moved, but does nothing to give them expression, then his emotions of remembrance and longing will be frustrated and unfulfilled, and he will feel a sense of deficiency in his ritual behavior. Therefore, the former kings established certain forms to be observed on such occasions so that men could fulfill their duty to honor those who deserve honor and show affection for those who command affection. Hence the sacrificial rites originate in the emotions of remembrance and longing, express the highest degree of loyalty, love, and reverence, and embody what is finest in ritual conduct and formal bearing. Only a sage can fully understand them. The sage understands them, the gentleman finds comfort in carrying them out, the officials are careful to maintain them, and the common people accept them as custom. To the gentleman they are a part of the way of man; to the common people they are something pertaining to the spirits.

Bells, drums, sounding stones, string and wind instruments, the musical compositions entitled "Shao," "Xia," "Hu," "Wu," "Zhuo," "Huan," "Xiao," and "Xiang"—these originate with the sudden changes of feeling of the gentleman and are the forms expressive of joy. The mourning garments and cane, the mourning hut and gruel, the mat of twigs and pillow of earth—these originate with the sudden changes of feeling of the gentleman and are forms expressive of grief and pain. The rules governing military expeditions, the gradations of punishment, which assure that no crime shall go unpunished—these originate with the sudden changes of feeling of the gentleman and are forms expressive of loathing and hatred.

When conducting a sacrifice, one divines to determine the appropriate day, fasts and purifies oneself, sets out the tables and mats with the offerings, and speaks to the invocator as though the spirit of the dead were really going to partake of the sacrifice. One takes up each of the offerings and presents them as though the spirit were really going to taste them. The server does not hold up the wine cup, but the sacrificer himself presents the wine vessel, as though the spirit were really going to drink from it. When the guests leave, the sacrificer bows and escorts them to the door, returns, changes his clothes, goes to his seat, and weeps as though the spirit had really departed along with them. How full of grief it is, how reverent! One serves the dead as though they were living, the departed as though present, giving body to the bodiless and thus fulfilling the proper forms of ceremony.

A DISCUSSION OF MUSIC

(Section 20)

Music is joy,[1] an emotion which man cannot help but feel at times. Since man cannot help feeling joy, his joy must find an outlet in voice and an expression in movement. The outcries and movements, and the inner emotional changes which occasion them, must be given full expression in accordance with the way of man. Man must have his joy, and joy must have its expression, but if that expression is not guided by the principles of the Way, then it will inevitably become disordered. The former kings hated such disorder, and therefore they created the musical forms of the odes and hymns in order to guide it. In this way they made certain that the voice would fully express the feelings of joy without becoming wild and abandoned, that the form would be well ordered but not unduly restrictive, that

---

[1]Xunzi's argument here and throughout the section is based upon the fact that the words *yue* (music) and *le* (joy) are written with the same character, a coincidence often exploited by early writers on music. By music, Xunzi means the entire musical performance, including singing, dancing, and musical accompaniment. Texts similar to this one on the nature of music, which agree closely with Xunzi's wording and views, are found in *Shiji* 24, "Treatise on Music," and *Liji*, sec. 19, "Record of Music."

the directness, complexity, intensity, and tempo of the musical performance would be of the proper degree to arouse the best in man's nature, and that evil and improper sentiments would find no opening to enter by. It was on this basis that the former kings created their music. And yet Mozi criticizes it. Why?[2]

When music is performed in the ancestral temple of the ruler, and the ruler and his ministers, superiors and inferiors, listen to it together, there are none who are not filled with a spirit of harmonious reverence. When it is performed within the household, and father and sons, elder and younger brothers listen to it together, there are none who are not filled with a spirit of harmonious kinship. And when it is performed in the community, and old people and young together listen to it, there are none who are not filled with a spirit of harmonious obedience. Hence music brings about complete unity and induces harmony. It arranges its accoutrements to comprise an adornment to moderation; it blends its performance to achieve the completion of form. It is sufficient to lead men in the single Way or to bring order to ten thousand changes. This is the manner in which the former kings created their music. And yet Mozi criticizes it. Why?

When one listens to the singing of the odes and hymns, his mind and will are broadened; when he takes up the shield and battle-ax and learns the postures of the war dance, his bearing acquires vigor and majesty; when he learns to observe the proper positions and boundaries of the dance stage and to match his movements with the accompaniment, he can move correctly in rank and his advancings and retirings achieve order. Music teaches men how to march abroad to punish offenders and how

---

[2]For Mozi's views on music, which he considered a waste of time and money, see *Mozi*, sec. 32, "Against Music."

to behave at home with courtesy and humility. Punishing offenders and behaving with courtesy and humility are based upon the same principle. If one marches abroad to punish offenders in accordance with the way learned through music, then there will be no one who will not obey and submit; if one behaves at home with courtesy and humility, then there will be no one who will not obey and be submissive. Hence music is the great arbiter of the world, the key to central harmony, and a necessary requirement of human emotion. This is the manner in which the former kings created their music. And yet Mozi criticizes it. Why?

Moreover, music was used by the former kings to give expression to their delight, and armies and weapons were used to give expression to their anger. The former kings were careful to show delight or anger only upon the correct occasions. Therefore, when they showed delight, the world joined with them in harmony, and when they showed anger, the violent and unruly shook with fear. The way of the former kings was to encourage and perfect rites and music, and yet Mozi criticizes such music. Therefore, I say that Mozi's attempts to teach the Way may be compared to a blind man trying to distinguish black from white, a deaf man trying to tell a clear tone from a muddy one, or a traveler trying to get to the state of Chu by journeying northward.

Music enters deeply into men and transforms them rapidly. Therefore, the former kings were careful to give it the proper form. When music is moderate and tranquil, the people become harmonious and shun excess. When music is stern and majestic, the people become well behaved and shun disorder. When the people are harmonious and well behaved, then the troops will be keen in striking power and the cities well guarded, and enemy states will not dare to launch an attack. In such a case, the common people will dwell in safety, take delight in their communities, and look up to their superiors with complete satisfaction.

Then the fame of the state will become known abroad, its glory
will shine forth greatly, and all people within the four seas will
long to become its subjects. Then at last a true king may be said
to have arisen.   *Music has to be a certain way*

   But if music is seductive and depraved, then the people will
become abandoned and mean-mannered. Those who are abandoned will fall into disorder; those who are mean-mannered will
fall to quarreling; and where there is disorder and quarreling,
the troops will be weak, the cities will revolt, and the state will
be menaced by foreign enemies. In such a case, the common
people will find no safety in their dwellings and no delight in
their communities, and they will feel only dissatisfaction toward
their superiors. Hence, to turn away from the proper rites and
music and to allow evil music to spread is the source of danger
and disgrace. For this reason the former kings honored the
proper rites and music and despised evil music. As I have said
before, it is the duty of the chief director of music to enforce the
ordinances and commands, to examine songs and writings, and
to abolish licentious music, attending to all matters at the appropriate time, so that strange and barbaric music is not allowed
to confuse the elegant classical modes.[3]

   Mozi claims that the sage kings rejected music and that the
Confucians are wrong to encourage it. But a gentleman will understand that this is not so. Music is something which the sage
kings found joy in, for it has the power to make good the hearts
of the people, to influence men deeply, and to reform their ways
and customs with facility. Therefore, the former kings guided
the people with rites and music, and the people became harmonious. If the people have emotions of love and hatred, but no
ways in which to express their joy or anger, then they will be-

---

[3]See above, p. 50.

come disordered. Because the former kings hated such disorder, they reformed the actions of the people and created proper music for them, and as a result the world became obedient. The fasting and mourning garments and the sound of lamenting and weeping cause the heart to be sad. The buckling on of armor and helmet, the songs sung as men march in rank cause the heart to be stirred[4] to valor. Seductive looks and the songs of Zheng and Wei[5] cause the heart to grow licentious, while the donning of court robes, sashes, and formal caps, the Shao dance, and the Wu song, cause the heart to feel brave and majestic. Therefore the gentleman does not allow his ears to listen to licentious sounds, his eyes to look at seductive beauty, or his mouth to speak evil words. These three things the gentleman is careful about. When depraved sounds move a man, they cause a spirit of rebellion to rise in him, and when such a spirit has taken shape, then disorder results. But when correct sounds move a man, they cause a spirit of obedience to rise, and when such a spirit has arisen, good order results. As singers blend their voices with that of the leader, so good or evil arise in response to the force that calls them forth. Therefore, the gentleman is careful to choose his environment.

The gentleman utilizes bells and drums to guide his will, and lutes and zithers to gladden his heart. In the movements of the war dance he uses shields and battle-axes; as decorations in the peace dance he uses feather ornaments and yak tails; and he sets the rhythm with sounding stones and woodwinds. Therefore, the purity of his music is modeled after Heaven, its breadth is modeled after the earth, and its posturings and turnings imitate

---

[4]Reading *tang* instead of *shang*.
[5]The songs of the regions of Zheng and Wei are famous in early literature for their licentious nature. See *Analects* XV, 10.

the four seasons. Hence, through the performance of music the will is made pure, and through the practice of rites the conduct is brought to perfection, the eyes and ears become keen, the temper becomes harmonious and calm, and customs and manners are easily reformed. All the world becomes peaceful and joins together in the joy of beauty and goodness. Therefore I say that music is joy. The gentleman takes joy in carrying out the Way; the petty man takes joy in gratifying his desires. He who curbs his desires in accordance with the Way will be joyful and free from disorder, but he who forgets the Way in the pursuit of desire will fall into delusion and joylessness. Therefore, music is the means of guiding joy, and the metal, stone, stringed, and bamboo instruments are the means of guiding virtue. When music is performed, the people will set their faces toward the true direction. Hence music is the most effective means to govern men. And yet Mozi criticizes it!

Music embodies an unchanging harmony, while rites represent unalterable reason. Music unites that which is the same; rites distinguish that which is different; and through the combination of rites and music the human heart is governed. To seek out the beginning and exhaust all change—this is the emotional nature of music; to illuminate the truth and do away with what is false—this is the essence of ritual. Because he criticized music, one would expect Mozi to have met with some punishment. And yet in his time the enlightened kings had all passed away and there was no one to correct his errors, so that stupid men continue to study his doctrines and bring jeopardy to themselves. The gentleman makes clear the nature of music—this is his virtue. But an age of disorder hates goodness and will not listen to the teachings of the gentleman, and alas, alas, they are left unfulfilled. Study the matter well, my students, and do not let yourselves be deluded!

This is the symbolism of music: the drum represents a vast pervasiveness; the bells represent fullness; the sounding stones represent restrained order; the mouth organs represent austere harmony; the flutes represent a spirited outburst; the ocarina and bamboo whistle represent breadth of tone; the zither represents gentleness; the lute represents grace; the songs represent purity and fulfillment; and the spirit of the dance joins with the Way of Heaven. The drum is surely the lord of music, is it not? Hence, it resembles Heaven, while the bells resemble earth, the sounding stones resemble water, the mouth organs and lutes resemble the sun, and the scrapers resemble the myriad beings of creation. How can one understand the spirit of the dance? The eyes cannot see it; the ears cannot hear it. And yet, when all the posturings and movements, all the steps and changes of pace are ordered and none are lacking in the proper restraint, when all the power of muscle and bone are brought into play, when all is matched exactly to the rhythm of the drums and bells and there is not the slightest awkwardness or discord—there is the spirit of the dance in all its manifold fullness and intensity!

When I observe the community drinking ceremony, I understand how gentle and easy the way of the true king can be.[6] The host goes in person to fetch the guest of honor and his attendants, and the other guests come of their own accord. This serves to make clear the distinction between eminent and humble. With three exchanges of light bows, the host and guest of honor move to the foot of the steps; after the guest has declined three times, the host leads him up the steps and bows low as he

---

[6]The following paragraph describes the traditional ritual observed at the *xiang* or community drinking ceremony held at the village school. Xunzi's description closely parallels that found in *Liji*, sec. 45, where the opening remark is attributed to Confucius. A much more detailed description of the ceremony is found in the *Yili*.

takes his seat. Between the host and the guest of honor there are many ceremonial offerings of the wine cup and many declinings, but with the guest's attendants the ceremony is much abbreviated. As for the other guests, they ascend, receive the cup of wine, take their seats, make obeisance to it, stand, drink it, and then, without returning the cup to the host, descend from the hall. Thus the complexity or simplicity of the ritual is adjusted to the distinctions of rank. The music master enters, ascends the steps, and sings three songs, after which the host presents him with a cup of wine. The player of the mouth organ enters, and from below the steps plays three songs, after which the host presents him with a cup of wine. The music master and mouth organ player then perform three songs in which they alternate with each other, and three songs in unison, and then the music master announces that the music is completed and retires. The host then orders two men to present the large wine tankard to the guest of honor and at the same time appoints a master of ceremonies. This indicates that it is possible to enjoy harmonious pleasure without any abandoned behavior. The guest of honor then presents the tankard to the host, the host presents it to the attendants of the guest of honor, and the attendants present it to the ordinary guests, each one drinking in the order of his age, until all is completed and the tankard is rinsed out. This indicates that it is possible to observe the distinctions of age and yet leave no one out of the drinking. After this, all descend, remove their shoes, ascend once more and sit down, after which everyone may drink as many cups as he wishes. Yet there must be moderation in the length of the drinking period; it should begin only after all morning duties have been completed, and should end before the time for evening duties. When the guest of honor departs, the host bows low and escorts him to the gate, and thus all ceremonies and forms are brought to an end. This indicates that it is possible to drink and feast without disorder. When the distinction between eminent and humble is made clear, when the complexity or simplicity of the ritual is adjusted to distinctions of rank, when there is harmonious pleasure without abandoned behavior, drinking according to distinctions of age but with no one left out, and drinking and feasting without disorder—when these five types of conduct are achieved, they will be sufficient to insure moral training to the individual and peace to the state, and when the state is peaceful, the world will be peaceful. Therefore I say that when I observe the community drinking ceremony, I understand how gentle and easy the way of the true king can be.

These are the signs of a disordered age: men wear bright-colored clothing, their manner is feminine, their customs are lascivious, their minds are set on profit, their conduct is erratic, their music is depraved, and their decorative arts are vile and garish. In satisfying the desires of the living they observe no limits, but in burying the dead they are mean and niggardly. They despise ritual principles and value daring and shows of strength. If they are poor, they steal, and if they are rich, they commit outrages. A well-ordered age is just the opposite of this.

DISPELLING OBSESSION[1]

(Section 21)

The thing that all men should fear is that they will become obsessed by a small corner of truth and fail to comprehend its overall principles. If they can correct this fault, they may return to correct standards, but if they continue to hesitate and be of two minds, then they will fall into delusion. There are not two Ways in the world; the sage is never of two minds. Nowadays the feudal lords follow different theories of government and the philosophers of the hundred schools teach different doctrines. Inevitably some teach what is right and some, what is wrong; some rulers govern well and others bring about disorder. Even the ruler of a chaotic state or the follower of a pernicious doctrine will undoubtedly in all sincerity seek what is proper and try to better his condition. But he is jealous and mistaken in his understanding of the Way and hence allows other men to lead him

---

[1]The word *bi* which is the keynote of Xunzi's discussion, denotes here a clouding or darkening of the faculties or the understanding, and Xunzi plays on the image of light and darkness throughout the chapter. The word "obsession" unfortunately does not fully convey the image of the original, but seems to come closest to expressing Xunzi's meaning.

astray. He clings to his familiar ways and is loath to hear them spoken ill of; he judges everything on the basis of his old prejudices; and when he encounters some different theory, he is loath to hear it praised. Thus he moves farther and farther away[2] from a condition of order, and yet never ceases to believe that he is doing right. Is this not what it means to be obsessed by a small corner of truth and to fail in the search for proper ways? If one fails to use his mind, then black and white may be right before his eyes and he will not see them; thunder or drums may be sounding in his ear and he will not hear them. How much more so with a man whose mind is obsessed![3] The man who has truly attained the Way is criticized from above by the rulers of chaotic states, and from below by men of pernicious doctrines. Is he not to be pitied?

What are the sources of obsession? One may be obsessed by desires or by hates, by the beginning of an affair or by the end, by those far away or those close by, by breadth of knowledge or by shallowness, by the past or by the present. When one makes distinctions among the myriad beings of creation, these distinctions all become potential sources of obsession. This is a danger in the use of the mind that is common to all men.

In ancient times there were rulers who were obsessed; Jie of the Xia dynasty and Zhou of the Yin are examples. Jie was obsessed by his favorite concubine Mo Xi and his counselor Si Guan and did not recognize the worth of Guan Longfeng. Thus his mind became deluded and his conduct disorderly. Zhou was obsessed by his favorite concubine Da Ji and his counselor Fei Lian and did not recognize the worth of Qi, the prince of Wei, and thus his mind became deluded and his conduct disorderly.

---

[2]Reading *li* instead of *sui*.
[3]Reading *bi* instead of *shi*.

Therefore, the courtiers of these two rulers abandoned the principles of loyal service and thought only of selfish aims, the common people hated and spoke ill of them and refused to obey their commands, and men of true worth retired from the court and went into hiding. Thus they lost possession of the Nine Provinces and brought desolation to the ancestral temples of their dynasties. Jie was driven to his death on Mount Li and Zhou's head ended dangling from the red pennant of his attacker. They could not foresee the future for themselves and no one was willing to reprimand them. Such are the disasters that come from obsession and a closed mind.

Cheng Tang took warning from the fate of Jie and therefore he was careful to employ his mind correctly and to govern with circumspection. Accordingly, he was able to benefit from the good advice of Yi Yin over a long period of time and did not depart from the Way. As a result he replaced Jie of the Xia as ruler and gained possession of the Nine Provinces. King Wen took warning from the fate of Zhou and therefore he was careful to employ his mind correctly and to govern with circumspection. Accordingly, he was able to benefit from the good advice of Lü Wang over a long period of time and did not depart from the Way. As a result he replaced Zhou of the Yin as ruler and gained possession of the Nine Provinces. The men of distant regions all came with rare gifts, so that these wise rulers had everything they wished for to please the eye, the ear, the mouth, and the palate; fair were the palaces they lived in and the fame which they enjoyed. While they lived the world sang songs of praise and when they died all within the four seas wept. This is what it means to reach the height of glory. The *Odes* says:

> The male and female phoenix sport and play,
> Their wings like shields,

Their voices like the sound of flutes.
Both male and female phoenixes come
To gladden the heart of the ruler.[4]

Such is the good fortune that comes from being free of obsession.

In ancient times there were subjects who were obsessed; Tang Yang and Xiqi are examples. Tang Yang was obsessed with a desire for power and drove Master Dai from the state.[5] Xiqi was obsessed with a desire for the throne and succeeded in casting suspicion upon Shensheng.[6] Tang Yang was executed in Song; Xiqi was executed in Jin.[7] One of them drove a worthy minister into exile; the other cast suspicion upon his brother. They ended by being executed and yet they did not have the understanding to foresee this end. Such are the disasters that come from obsession and a closed mind. Thus, from ancient times to the present there has never been a man whose conduct was marked by greed, treason, and a struggle for power, and who yet did not suffer shame and destruction.

Bao Shu, Ning Qi, and Xi Peng were benevolent, wise, and free from obsession. Therefore, they were able to give their support to Guan Zhong and to enjoy a fame and fortune that were

---

[4]No such verse is found in the present text of the *Odes*.

[5]Tang Yang is mentioned in *Lü shi chunqiu*, ch. 2, *Dangran*, and ch. 18, *Yinci*, as an evil adviser to King Kang, the infamous last ruler of the state of Song, who was killed by his enemies in 286 B.C. Master Dai is identified with Dai Busheng, a minister of Song mentioned in *Mencius* IIIB, 6.

[6]Xiqi was a son of Duke Xian of Jin by the duke's second consort, Lady Li. He and his mother succeeded in bringing about the downfall of the heir apparent, Shensheng, by making it appear that he was attempting to poison the duke. As a result, Shensheng committed suicide in 656 B.C. See *Zuozhuan*, Duke Xi 4th year.

[7]Xiqi was killed in 651 B.C. by a high minister of Jin. The date of Tang Yang's death is unknown, but it was during the reign of King Kang.

equal to his.[8] Shao Gong and Lü Wang were benevolent, wise, and free from obsession. Therefore, they were able to give their support to the duke of Zhou and to enjoy a fame and fortune that were equal to his.[9] This is what the old text means when it says, "To recognize the worthy is called enlightenment; to aid the worthy is called ability. Work hard, work diligently at it, and you will surely receive long-lasting fortune." Such is the good fortune that comes from being free of obsession.

Among the itinerant philosophers of former times there were men who were obsessed; the followers of pernicious doctrines are an example. Mozi was obsessed by utilitarian considerations and did not understand the beauties of form. Songzi was obsessed by the need to lessen desires, for he did not understand how they could be satisfied. Shenzi was obsessed with the concept of law and did not understand the part to be played by worthy men. Shen Buhai was obsessed by the power of circumstance and did not understand the role of the human intelligence.[10] Huizi was obsessed by words and did not understand the truth that lies behind them. Zhuangzi was obsessed by thoughts of Heaven [i.e., Nature] and did not understand the importance of man. He who thinks only of utilitarian concerns will take the Way to be wholly a matter of material profit. He who thinks only of desires will take the Way to be wholly a matter of physical satisfaction. He

---

[8]Bao Shu, Ning Qi, and Xi Peng were ministers of Duke Huan of Qi who assisted the famous Guan Zhong in building up the power of the state. See above, p. 40, n. 8.

[9]Shao Gong Shi and Taigong Lü Wang were virtuous ministers to the duke of Zhou who are frequently mentioned in the *Book of Documents*. They became the founders of the ruling houses of Yan and Qi respectively.

[10]Songzi preached a life of frugality and few desires; Shenzi was a Daoist–Legalist thinker. See above, p. 92, nn. 11 and 12. Shen Buhai was one of the founders of the Legalist school.

who thinks only of law will take the Way to be wholly a matter of policy. He who thinks only of circumstance will take the Way to be wholly a matter of expedience. He who thinks only of words will take the Way to be wholly a matter of logic. He who thinks only of Heaven will take the Way to be wholly a matter of harmonizing with natural forces. These various doctrines comprehend only one small corner of the Way, but the true Way must embody constant principles and be capable of embracing all changes. A single corner of it will not suffice. These men with their limited understanding saw one corner of the Way and, failing to understand that it was only a corner, they considered it sufficient and proceeded to expound it in engaging terms. Such men bring chaos to themselves and delusion to others; if they are in a superior position, they inflict their obsessions upon their inferiors; and if in an inferior position, they inflict them upon their superiors. Such are the disasters that come from obsession and a closed mind.

Confucius, on the other hand, was benevolent, wise, and free from obsession. Thus, although he studied the doctrines of the various other schools, he established his own school, taught the way of the Zhou, and showed how it could be put into practice, for he was not obsessed by old habits and prejudices. Hence his virtue is equal to that of the duke of Zhou, and his fame matches that of the sage kings of the Three Dynasties. Such is the good fortune that comes from being free of obsession.

The sage understands the dangers involved in improper use of the mind, and sees the disasters that come from obsession and a closed mind. Therefore, he does not allow himself to be influenced by considerations of desire or hate, beginning or end, distance or nearness, breadth or shallowness, past or present, but searches and examines all things and weighs them impartially in a balance. As a result, the distinctions which exist in all things cannot inflict obsession upon him and bring disorder to his reason. And what is the balance that he uses? It is the Way. The mind must understand the Way, for if it does not, it will reject the Way and give approval to that which is at variance with it. And what man, seeking to gratify his desires, will abide by what he has rejected and refuse to follow what he has given his approval to? Thus, if a man whose mind has rejected the Way sets out to select helpers, he will invariably find himself drawn to men whose conduct is at variance with the Way, and will not appreciate men who abide by it. When a man whose mind has rejected the Way joins with similar men to criticize those who abide by the Way, this is the beginning of disorder. How can such conduct represent true understanding?

The mind must first understand the Way before it can approve it, and it must first approve it before it can abide by it and reject what is at variance with it. If a man whose mind has given approval to the Way sets out to select helpers, he will find himself drawn to men whose conduct is in accordance with the Way and will feel no affinity for men whose conduct is at variance with it. And when a man whose mind has given approval to the Way joins with similar men to criticize those whose conduct is at variance with the Way, then this is the starting point of orderly government. Why should such a man need to worry about how true his understanding is? Therefore the beginning of good government lies in understanding the Way.

How does a man understand the Way? Through the mind. And how can the mind understand it? Because it is empty, unified, and still. The mind is constantly storing up things, and yet it is said to be empty. The mind is constantly marked by diversity, and yet it is said to be unified. The mind is constantly moving, and yet it is said to be still. Man is born with an intellect, and where there is intellect there is memory. Memory is what is stored up in the mind. Yet the mind is said to be empty because what has already been stored up in it does not hinder the reception of new impressions. Therefore it is said to be empty. Man is born with an intellect, and where there is intellect there is an awareness of differences. An awareness of differences means that one can have an understanding of a variety of facts at the same time, and where there is such understanding, there is diversity. And yet the mind is said to be unified because it does not allow the understanding of one fact to impinge upon that of another. Therefore it is said to be unified. When the mind is asleep, it produces dreams; when it is unoccupied, it wanders off in idle fancy; and if allowed to do so, it will produce from these all manner of plots and schemes. Hence the mind is constantly moving. And yet it is said to be still, because it does not allow such dreams and noisy fancies to disorder its understanding. Therefore it is said to be still.

A man who has not yet attained the Way but is seeking it should be urged to take emptiness, unity, and stillness as his guides. If he who seeks to abide by the Way has emptiness, then he may enter into it; if he who seeks to serve the Way has unity, then he may master it; if he who seeks to meditate on the Way has stillness, then he may perceive it.[11] He who understands the Way and perceives its nature, he who understands the Way and carries it out, may be said to embody the Way. Emptiness, unity, and stillness—these are the qualities of great and pure enlightenment.

When a man has such enlightenment, there are none of the myriad beings of creation that have form and yet are not perceived by it, none that are perceived and yet not comprehended, none that are comprehended and yet not assigned to their prop-

---

[11]The text is hardly intelligible at this point and is probably garbled or defective. I have followed Kanaya in the translation of the first two sentences of this paragraph, though the interpretation is highly tentative.

er places. He who has such enlightenment may sit in his room and view the entire area within the four seas, may dwell in the present and yet discourse on distant ages. He has a penetrating insight into all beings and understands their true nature, studies the ages of order and disorder and comprehends the principle behind them. He surveys all heaven and earth, governs all beings, and masters the great principle and all that is in the universe. Broad and vast—who knows the limits of such a man? Brilliant and comprehensive—who knows his virtue? Shadowy and ever-changing—who knows his form? His brightness matches the sun and moon; his greatness fills the eight directions. Such is the Great Man. How could he become the victim of obsession?

The mind is the ruler of the body and the master of its god-like intelligence. It gives commands, but it is not subject to them. Of its own volition it prohibits or permits, snatches or accepts, goes or stops. Thus the mouth can be forced to speak or to be silent; the body can be forced to crouch or to extend itself; but the mind cannot be made to change its opinion. What it considers right it will accept; what it considers wrong it will reject. Hence we may say that it is the nature of the mind that no prohibition may be placed upon its selections. Inevitably it will see things for itself. And although the objects it perceives may be many and diverse, if its acuity is of the highest level, it cannot become divided within itself. The *Odes* says:

> I pick and pick the burr-weed
> But it does not fill my slanting basket.
> I sigh for my loved one;
> I would be in the ranks of Zhou.[12]

---

[12]"Airs of Zhounan," *Juaner*, Mao text no. 3. I have interpreted the last line differently from Karlgren in order to make it fit Xunzi's remarks.

A slanting basket is easy enough to fill, and burr-weed is easy enough to gather. And yet she never succeeds in filling the basket because her mind is divided between her work and her loved one in the ranks of Zhou.

Therefore it is said that, if the mind is distracted, it will lack understanding; if it is unbalanced, it will lack acuity; and if it is divided, it will fall into doubt and delusion. But if it avoids these three conditions and examines and compares correctly, then it can understand all things, while the body, having mastered all actions, will achieve beauty.

As a basis for action, diversity is impractical. Hence the wise man selects one thing and unifies his actions about it. The farmer is well versed in the work of the fields, but he cannot become a director of agriculture. The merchant is well versed in the ways of the market, but he cannot become a director of commerce. The artisan is well versed in the process of manufacture, but he cannot become a director of crafts. Yet there are men who, though they possess none of these three skills, are still able to fill the offices that direct them. This is not because they are well versed in the facts, but because they are well versed in the Way.[13] He who is well versed in the facts alone will treat each fact as a fact and no more. He who is well versed in the Way will unify his treatment of the facts. Hence, the gentleman finds a basis for unity in the Way and on this basis examines and compares the facts. Since he has the unity of the Way as his basis, his approach will be correct; and since he examines and compares the facts, his perception will be clear. With thinking that is based upon a correct approach and action that is based upon clear perception, he is able to control all things.

In ancient times, when Shun governed the world, he did not issue detailed commands concerning each matter and yet all

---

[13]Adding a *fei* before the *jing* of the second clause.

things were brought to completion. He clung to a single attitude of fearful caution and his glory became replete. He nourished an attitude of subtle watchfulness and achieved glory, though few men understood why. Hence the Classic of the Way[14] says, "There should be a fearfulness in the mind of man; there should be subtlety of vision in the mind of the Dao." One must have the enlightenment of a gentleman before he can comprehend the signs of such fearfulness and subtlety.

The mind may be compared to a pan of water. If you place the pan on a level and do not jar it, then the heavy sediment will settle to the bottom and the clear water will collect on top, so that you can see your beard and eyebrows in it and examine the lines of your face. But if a faint wind passes over the top of the water, the heavy sediment will be stirred up from the bottom and the clear water will become mingled with it, so that you can no longer get a clear reflection of even a large object. The mind is the same way. If you guide it with reason, nourish it with clarity, and do not allow external objects to unbalance it, then it will be capable of determining right and wrong and of resolving doubts. But if you allow petty external objects to pull it about, so that its proper form becomes altered and its inner balance is upset, then it will not be capable of making even gross distinctions.

Many men have loved the art of writing, but Cang Jie alone is honored by later ages as its master, because he concentrated upon it.[15] Many men have loved husbandry, but Lord Millet alone is honored by later ages as its master, because he concentrated upon

---

[14]Nothing is known of this work. The same quotation, with only slight textual variation, appears in the "Plan of Great Yu" of the *Documents*. But this chapter is a later forgery, so that this passage in Xunzi probably represents the earliest source of the quotation.

[15]The men mentioned in this paragraph are all mythical or semimythical culture heroes of the distant past.

it. Many men have loved music, but Kui alone is honored by later ages as its master, because he concentrated upon it. Many men have loved righteousness, but Shun alone is honored by later ages as its master, because he concentrated upon it. Chui invented bows and Fouyou invented arrows, but it remained for Yi to master the art of archery. Xizhong invented carriages and Chengdu discovered how to use horses to pull them, but it remained for Zaofu to perfect the art of carriage driving. Hence, from ancient times to the present there has never been a man who attained mastery by trying to attend to a diversity of things at one time. Zengzi[16] said, "Any man who, while he is trying to sing, is at the same time wondering if he can swat the mouse sitting on the corner of his mat is not going to join in a chorus of mine!"

There was a man who lived in a cave, and his name was Ji.[17] He was good at thinking up riddles and liked to meditate. But if his eyes or ears were aroused by any stimulus, his thoughts became distracted, and if he heard the buzzing of mosquitoes or flies, it destroyed his concentration. Therefore he withdrew himself from all stimulus and went where he would be far away from the buzzing of mosquitoes and flies, and there, living in quietude and calm meditation, he perfected his art. If he had meditated as intensively on benevolence, would he not have achieved real subtlety? Mencius was shocked at his wife's behavior and turned her out of the house.[18] This shows remarkable

---

[16]A disciple of Confucius often mentioned in the *Analects*.

[17]The pronunciation of this character is unknown. I have romanized it according to the phonetic.

[18]According to the version of the story in *Hanshi waizhuan* 9, Mencius came into his wife's room unannounced and found her sprawled in an unladylike position. In that version, however, he did not succeed in turning her out, but on the contrary was severely reprimanded by his mother for walking in on people unannounced.

strength of will, but not very much thought.[19] Confucius's disciple You Zi hated the thought of falling asleep and so he burned the palm of his hand to keep himself awake. This shows remarkable endurance, but not very much concern for the body. To withdraw oneself from all stimulus and go where one will be far away from the buzzing of mosquitoes and flies can be called cautious fearfulness, but not subtlety. True subtlety is the quality of the perfect man. What has he to do with strength of will, endurance, and fearfulness? A dull brightness shines about his exterior, and a clear brightness within him. The sage follows his desires, satisfies all his emotions, and at the same time is restrained, because he possesses reason. What has he to do with strength of will, endurance, or fearfulness? The benevolent man practices the Way through inaction; the sage practices the Way through nonstriving. The thoughts of the benevolent man are reverent; the thoughts of the sage are joyous. This is the way to govern the mind.

When you observe objects, doubts arise, and if your inner mind does not settle them, then your perception of external objects will become unclear. And if your thoughts themselves are unclear, then you cannot settle the doubts that arise. A man walking along a dark road will mistake a stone lying on its side for a crouching tiger, or a row of trees for a file of men following him. This is because the darkness obscures his vision. A drunken man will try to leap a ditch a hundred paces wide as though it were a narrow gutter, or will stoop to go through a city gate as though it were a low doorway. This is because the wine has disordered his spirit. If you press your eyeball when you look at something, you will see two objects instead of one; if you cup

---

[19]The order of the text is somewhat jumbled at this point, and I have followed Kanaya's rearrangement and interpretation.

your hands over your ears, dull noises will sound like a sharp din. This is because the actions you take disorder the functioning of the faculties. If you look down on a herd of cows from the top of a hill, they will look no bigger than sheep, and yet no one hoping to find sheep is likely to run down the hill after them. It is simply that the distance obscures their actual size. If you look up at a forest from the foot of a hill, the biggest trees appear no taller than chopsticks, and yet no one hoping to find chopsticks is likely to go picking among them. It is simply that the height obscures their actual dimensions. When water is moving and its reflections waver, men do not use it as a mirror to judge beauty by, for they know that it is the nature of such water to cast deceptive reflections. When a blind man looks up at the sky and declares that he sees no stars, men do not use his declaration to decide whether stars really exist or not, for they know that his faculties are impaired. Anyone who would actually base his judgments upon such evidence would be the biggest fool in the world. Such a fool in his judgments uses what is already doubtful to try to settle further doubts, and hence his judgments are never accurate. And if his judgments are not accurate, how can he hope to escape error?

There was a man named Juan Shuliang who lived south of Xiashou. He was stupid and easily frightened. One night he was walking in the moonlight when, glancing down and seeing his shadow, he took it for a crouching ghost. Looking up, he caught sight of his own hair and took it for a devil standing over him. He whirled around and started running, and when he reached his home he fell unconscious and died. Is this not sad? Always when people see ghosts, it is at times when they are aroused and excited, and they make their judgments in moments when their faculties are confused and blinded. At such times they affirm that what exists does not exist, or that what does not exist exists, and then they consider the matter settled. A man, having contracted a chill from the dampness, proceeds to beat a drum and make an offering of a pig in hopes of effecting a cure.[20] He wears out the drum and loses a pig in the process, that is certain, but no blessing of recovery follows as a result. Thus, although he may not happen to live south of Xiashou, he is no different from the man I have described above.

On the whole, by understanding the nature of man, you can understand the principles that govern all other beings. But if, having understood human nature, you seek thereby to understand the principles of other beings, but fail to set any limit to your search, then you may spend all the rest of your life without reaching any fulfillment. You may try a million different ways of mastering these principles, but in the end you will still not be able to understand all the transformations which the countless beings undergo, and you will be no different from an ignorant man. Anyone who studies until he himself is old and his sons are full grown, and yet neither advances beyond the stage of the ignorant man nor has the sense to give up—such a man may be called a real fool. Learning must always have a stopping place. Where should it stop? It should stop with the point of complete sufficiency. What do I mean by complete sufficiency? I mean the understanding of the sage and the king.[21] The sage has complete mastery of all moral principles; the king has complete mastery of all regulations of society. Those who possess these two kinds of mastery are worthy to be called the pinnacles of the world. Hence the scholar should take the sage and the king as his teachers. He should take their regulations as his model and, on the

---

[20]The text is slightly garbled at this point. I have followed Kanaya's rearrangement and interpretation.

[21]Adding the word "king," which has dropped out here.

basis of this model, seek to penetrate their reasoning and work to become like them. He who strives for this ideal is a man of breeding, he who comes close to realizing it is a gentleman, and he who truly understands it is a sage. He who has understanding but fails to make his plans on the basis of this ideal may be called rapacious.[22] He who has bravery but fails to support this ideal may be called a brigand. He who has keen perception but fails to comprehend this ideal may be called mechanical minded. He who has much talent but fails to practice this ideal may be called wily. He who is clever at talking but fails to speak of this ideal may be called a blabbermouth. The old text says, "There are two things it is important to do in the world: to perceive the right in what men consider wrong, and to perceive the wrong in what men consider right." In other words, you must judge what things conform to the king's regulations and what do not.

Certainly there are those in the world who do not accept this ideal of the sage and the king as the highest norm, but can they possibly claim still to be able to distinguish right from wrong, or to separate the crooked from the straight? And if they cannot distinguish right from wrong, or separate crooked from straight, if they cannot tell the difference between order and disorder, or practice the way that is proper to mankind, then, although they may have other abilities, it will be no profit to anyone, and if they are without ability it will be no one's loss. Such men do nothing but propound strange theories, toy with unusual language, and vex and confuse others. Offensively aggressive and glib, brazen-faced and impervious to shame, willful in conduct and indifferent to right, rash in judgment and with an eye out for profit alone, they have no use for humility, no respect for propriety, but are concerned only in getting the better of their opponents. Such are the ways of evil men whose

---

[22]Reading *jue* instead of *ju*.

theories bring disorder to the age, and yet how many of the propounders of theories in the world today are like this! This is what the old text means when it says, "The gentleman despises those who consider perception to consist merely in the analysis of words, or discrimination to consist merely in the description of objects. The gentleman despises men of broad learning and powerful memory who yet do not conform to the regulations of the king."

Things which are of no help to you in fulfilling your undertakings, no help to you in obtaining what you seek, no help to you in escaping from what you dread—put such things far away from yourself and reject them. Do not allow them to impede you; do not harbor them in your breast even for a moment. Do not long for the past, do not fret over the future, and do not allow your mind to be disturbed by anxiety or miserliness. Act when the time comes; respond to things as they appear; judge events as they occur; and the distinction between order and disorder, proper and improper will become abundantly clear.

There has never been an enlightened ruler who succeeded by keeping secrets from his ministers but failed by being too frank with them. There has never been an unenlightened ruler who succeeded by being open with his ministers but failed by hiding things from them.[23] If the ruler of men is too secretive, then only slanderous reports will reach his ears and honest advisers will fall silent. Petty men will draw close to him and gentlemen will depart. The *Odes* says:

> He mistakes darkness for light
> And foxes and badgers have their way.[24]

---

[23]Because an enlightened ruler by definition attracts good ministers and an unenlightened one by definition attracts bad ministers.

[24]No such lines are found in the present text of the *Odes*.

This refers to a situation in which the ruler is sunk in delusion and his ministers are evil. But if the ruler is open with his ministers, then honest advice will reach his ears and slanderous reports will cease. Gentlemen will draw close to him and petty men will depart. The *Odes* says:

> Bright and enlightened are those below;
> Bright and glorious is the one above.[25]

This refers to a situation in which the ruler is enlightened and his ministers are transformed to virtue.

---

[25]"Greater Odes," *Daming*, Mao text no. 236. I have interpreted the lines differently from Karlgren in order to make them fit Xunzi's comment.

(Section 22)

This is the way the true kings of later times fixed the names of things. In the case of legal terms, they followed the practices of the Yin dynasty; in the case of terms pertaining to ranks and titles, they followed Zhou practice; and for the names of ceremonies and ceremonial objects, they followed ritual practice. For the common names applied to all the various things of creation, they followed the established customs of China, and made certain that such names could be used in distant regions whose customs are different, so that a common means of communication could be established thereby.

These are the common names that apply to man. That which is as it is from the time of birth is called the nature of man. That which is harmonious from birth, which is capable of perceiving through the senses and of responding to stimulus spontaneously

---

[1]The title of the section is taken from *Analects* XIII, 3, where Confucius discusses the need to rectify names. It is Xunzi's answer to Hui Shi, Gongsun Long, and the other philosophers of the School of Names. It presents many difficulties of interpretation, and the translation is therefore tentative at many points. On the whole, I have followed Kanaya's interpretation, though I do not always adopt his emendations.

and without effort, is also called the nature. The likes and dislikes, delights and angers, griefs and joys of the nature are called
emotions. When the emotions are aroused and the mind makes
a choice from among them, this is called thought. When the
mind conceives a thought and the body[2] puts it into action, this
is called conscious activity. When the thoughts have accumulated sufficiently, the body is well trained, and then the action is
carried to completion, this is also called conscious activity. When
one acts from considerations of profit, it is called business. When
one acts from considerations of duty, it is called [moral] conduct.
The faculty which allows man to have understanding is called
knowledge. Understanding which has practical applicability is
also called knowledge. The understanding which makes man capable of something is called ability. Capability which has practical application is also called ability. Injuries to the nature are
called sickness; unexpected occurrences which one meets with
are called fate. These are the common names that apply to man,
the names that have been fixed by the kings of later times.

When the king sets about regulating names, if the names and
the realities to which they apply are made fixed and clear, so that
he can carry out the Way and communicate his intentions to
others, then he may guide the people with circumspection and
unify them. Hence to split words and recklessly make up new
names, throwing the names that have already been established
into confusion, leading the people into doubt and delusion, and
causing men to argue and contend with each other is a terrible
evil and should be punished in the same way that one punishes
those who tamper with tallies or weights and measures. If so,
then the people will not dare to think up pretexts for using
strange words and throwing the established names into disorder,

---

[2]Reading *tai* instead of *neng* here and in the next sentence.

but will become simple and honest. When the people are simple and honest, they are easy to employ, and when they are easy to employ, then much can be accomplished. Again, because the people do not dare to think up pretexts for using strange words and throwing the established names into disorder, they will be of one mind in obeying the law, and will be careful to follow orders, and if they are like that, the ruler's accomplishments will be long lasting. When the ruler's accomplishments are long lasting and his undertakings are brought to completion, this is the height of good government. All of this is the result of being careful to see that men stick to the names which have been agreed upon.

Nowadays, however, the sages and true kings have all passed away. Men are careless in abiding by established names, strange words come into use, names and realities become confused, and the distinction between right and wrong has become unclear. Even the officials who guard the laws or the scholars who recite the Classics have all become confused. If a true king were to appear now, he would surely set about reviving the old names, and creating new ones as they were needed. To do so, he would have to examine carefully to see why names are needed, how to go about distinguishing between things that are the same and those that are different, and what essential standards should be used in regulating names.

[If there are no fixed names,] but men begin to discriminate the different forms of things on the basis of their own particular observations, each applying his own names and interpreting the different phenomena in his own fashion, then the relationships between names and realities will become obscured and entangled, the distinction between eminent and humble will become unclear, and men will no longer discriminate properly between things that are the same and those that are different. In such a case there will be a real danger that the ruler's intentions will not be properly communicated and understood, and his undertakings will undoubtedly be plagued with difficulty and failure. For this reason the wise man is careful to set up the proper distinctions and to regulate names so that they will apply correctly to the realities they designate. In this way he makes clear the distinction between eminent and humble and discriminates properly between things that are the same and those that are different. If this is done, there will be no danger that the ruler's intentions will be improperly communicated and understood, and his undertakings will suffer no difficulties or failure. This is the reason why correct names are needed.

And how does one go about distinguishing between things that are the same and those that are different? One relies upon the senses. Things which are of the same species and form will be apprehended by the senses as being all the same thing. Therefore, after comparing such things with other things of a similar nature, one may settle upon a common designation. In this way one arrives at a common name for all the things of one class, which everyone agrees to use when the occasion demands. Differences in shape, color, or marking are distinguished by the eye. Differences of tone, timbre, pitch, or modulation are distinguished by the ear. Sweetness, bitterness, saltiness, blandness, sharpness, sourness, and other variations in flavor are distinguished by the mouth. The perfumes of incense and flowery fragrance, rankness, rancidness, putridness, and other variations of odor are distinguished by the nose. Pain, itchiness, cold, heat, smoothness, roughness, lightness, and heaviness are distinguished by the body. Speech, events, delight, anger, grief, joy, love, hate, and desire are distinguished by the mind. In addition the mind possesses an overall understanding. Because of this overall understanding, it may rely upon the data of the ear and understand sounds correctly or rely upon the data of the eye and understand forms correctly. But this overall understanding must always wait until it has received new data from the senses and matched it with the data already recorded in the mind concerning a particular class of objects, before it can arrive at a correct understanding of the object. If a man simply allows his senses to record data but does not attempt to understand what they have recorded, or if he reaches an overall understanding of the phenomenon but cannot put it into words, then everyone will call him an ignorant man. The above explains the way in which one goes about distinguishing between things that are the same and those that are different.

When this has been done, then one may begin assigning names accordingly. Things that are the same should have the same name; those that are different should have different names. Where a single name is sufficient to express the meaning, a single name should be used; where a single name is not sufficient to express the meaning, a compound name should be used. Where there is no conflict between the single name and the compound name, they may be used interchangeably to refer to the same thing as occasion demands. Although they are used interchangeably, there is no harm done.[3] Because one understands that different realities must have different names, one sees to it that they are given different names. There must be no confusion about this, any more than about the necessity to see to it that all things which are the same in reality have the same name.

---

[3]Xunzi is replying to Gongsun Long's famous conundrum, "A white horse is not a horse." Horse is the single name, white horse the compound name, but the fact that one uses "horse" at one time and "white horse" at another does not mean that a white horse is not also a horse.

The myriad beings of creation are countless, and yet at times we wish to refer to all of them in general, and so we call them "things." "Things" is the broadest general term. One starts with a limited general term and keeps moving on to broader and broader general terms until one can go no farther, and there one stops. At other times we wish to refer to particular categories of things, and so we use words like "bird" or "beast." These are broad particular terms. One starts with the broadest possible term and moves on to terms whose meaning is more and more circumscribed until one can go no farther, and there one stops.

Names have no intrinsic appropriateness. One agrees to use a certain name and issues an order to that effect, and if the agreement is abided by and becomes a matter of custom, then the name may be said to be appropriate, but if people do not abide by the agreement, then the name ceases to be appropriate. Names have no intrinsic reality. One agrees to use a certain name and issues an order that it shall be applied to a certain reality, and if the agreement is abided by and becomes a matter of custom, then it may be said to be a real name. There are, however, names which are intrinsically good. Names which are clear, simple, and not at odds with the thing they designate may be said to be good names.

There are things which share the same form but occupy different places and things which have different forms but occupy the same place.[4] One must be careful to distinguish between them. Things which share the same form but occupy different places may be referred to by the same name, though they are actually two different realities. There are things which change their form and, although they are still the same thing in reality,

---

[4] E.g., two horses in different places, or a single man who has one form in youth and another in old age.

appear to become something different.[5] These are called transformed things. Although they change form, they are not distinguished anew because they are actually the same in reality. This
is how one should go about examining realities and assigning
designations. These are the essential standards to be used in regulating names. One must be careful to examine the way in which
the kings of later times fixed the names of things.

"It is no shame to suffer insult." "The sage has no love for
himself." "When you kill a thief, you do not kill a man."[6] Men
who make statements like these are deluded in their use of words
and bring confusion to names. If one examines into the reasons
why names are needed and determines which names are appropriate, he can put a stop to such statements. "Mountains and
chasms are on the same level." "It is the emotional nature of man
to have few desires." "A feast of grass-fed and grain-fed animals
adds nothing to the delight of the palate; the music of the great
bell adds nothing to one's joy."[7] Men who make statements such
as these are deluded in their understanding of realities and bring
confusion to names. If one examines them in the light of what I
have said about how to differentiate between same and different,[8]
and determines which names fit the situation, then he can put a

---

[5]Xunzi is probably referring to such transformations as those of a silkworm or a
cicada.

[6]The first of these statements is attributed in sec. 18 of the *Xunzi* to Song Jian (see
above, p. 92, n. 12). The second is probably a reference to Mozi's doctrine of universal love. The third is found in *Mozi*, sec. 45.

[7]The first statement is one of the paradoxes of Hui Shi, recorded in *Zhuangzi*, sec.
33 (where it reads "Mountains and marshes are on the same level"). The second is
attributed in *Xunzi*, sec. 18, to Song Jian. The third probably refers to Mozi's attacks on music and luxurious living.

[8]I.e., one should check statements such as "mountains and chasms are on the same
level" against the data of the senses. Following Kanaya, I read *er* instead of *wu* in
the first clause.

stop to such statements. "Deny and make a visit." "The pillar has an ox." "A white horse is not a horse."[9] Men who make statements like these are deluded in their use of words and bring confusion to realities. If one examines them in the light of the agreed usage of names, accepts those which fit in with agreed usage, and rejects those that depart from it, he can put a stop to such statements. All the pernicious theories and inane sayings which men willfully concoct and which depart from the proper way can be classified under these three types of delusion. The enlightened ruler understands these classifications and does not argue with men who make such statements.

It is easy to unify the people by means of the Way, though one cannot expect them to share in the process of direction.[10] Therefore, the enlightened ruler controls them with power, guides them with the Way, encourages their advancements with commands, brings enlightenment to them through the teaching of ethical relations, and prohibits evil through punishments. Hence his people are converted to the Way as though by supernatural power. What need has he of persuasive speaking?[11] But now the sages and true kings have passed away and the world is in confusion. Evil doctrines arise, and the gentleman has no power to control the people with and no punishments to prohibit them from evil. Therefore, he must have recourse to persuasive speaking.

Names are used when the reality itself is not clearly understood. Combinations of names are used when single names

---

[9]The meaning and origin of the first two statements is unknown. In the third, the word "white" has dropped out of the text.

[10]Compare this with *Analects* VIII, 9: "The Master (Confucius) said, 'The people may be made to follow a path of action, but they may not be made to understand it.'"

[11]Reading *shui* instead of *shi*.

alone are not understood. Explanations are used when combinations of names alone are not understood. Discourses are used when simple explanations alone are not understood. Hence, names, combinations of names, explanations, and discourses are the major forms to be used in conducting practical affairs and are the basis of the king's business. When one, on hearing the names, can immediately understand the realities they refer to, then names are fulfilling their practical function. When they are combined to create pleasing forms, then they are fulfilling their esthetic function. He who can use names in such a way that they are both practical and esthetically pleasing may be said to have a real understanding of them.

Names are the means by which one attempts to distinguish different realities.[12] Phrases consist of combinations of names for different realities, put together so as to express a single meaning. Discourses and explanations are the means by which, without allowing names to become separated from realities, one makes men understand the principles of correct action. Names and combinations of names are the instruments of discourse and explanation. Discourse and explanation are the means by which the mind gives form to the Way. The mind is the supervisor of the Way, and the Way is the foundation of good government. The mind should be in accord with the Way, explanations in accord with the mind, and phrases in accord with explanations; the correct names should be formed into combinations; understanding should be based upon the true circumstances; differences should be carefully distinguished without error; and analogies should be drawn which are not forced or false. When one listens to the words of others, one should bring them into accord with the proper forms; when one discourses on one's

---

[12]Reading *yi* instead of *lei*.

own ideas, one should give a complete explanation of one's reasons. If one employs the correct way in order to distinguish what is false, just as one stretches a line to distinguish between crooked and straight, then pernicious theories will be powerless to cause confusion and the doctrines of the hundred schools will have nowhere to hide.

The sage has the understanding that comes from listening to many things, but does not let pride show in his face; he has the kind of generosity that embraces many men, but does not let it appear that he boasts of his virtue. When his doctrines are practiced, the world is upright; when they are not, he strives to make clear the Way but hides his person. These are the characteristics of the sage's discourse. This is what the *Odes* means when it says:

> Gracious and splendid,
> Like a jade scepter, a jade baton,
> Of good fame, good aspect,
> The joyous gentleman
> Is regulator of the four quarters.[13]

The gentleman and man of breeding observes the proper degree of courtesy and obeys the rules of seniority. No improper words leave his lips; no evil sayings come from his mouth. With a benevolent mind he explains his ideas to others, with the mind of learning he listens to their words, and with a fair mind he makes his judgments. He is not moved by the censure or praise of the mob; he does not try to bewitch[14] the ears and eyes of his observers; he does not cringe before the power and authority of eminent men; he does not feign delight in the words of the

---

[13]"Greater Odes," *Quane*, Mao text no. 252.
[14]Reading *ye* instead of *zhi*.

ruler's favorites.[15] Therefore he can abide by the Way and not be of two minds, can endure hardship[16] without betraying his ideals, and can enjoy good fortune without overstepping the bounds of good conduct. He honors what is fair and upright and despises meanness and wrangling. Such is the discourse of the gentleman and the man of breeding. This is what the *Odes* means when it says:

> The long night passes slowly;
> Long thoughts beset me.
> If I am not false to antiquity
> Nor to the principles of ritual,
> Why fear what men say?[17]

The words of the gentleman are far-ranging and detailed, apt and to the point, varied and yet unified. He employs the correct names and chooses suitable phrases in order to insure that his meaning is clear. His words and phrases act as the messengers of his meaning. He makes certain that they are sufficient to communicate his thoughts, and there he stops, for to try to force them to do more would be evil. If the names one uses are sufficient to indicate the realities one has in mind, and the phrases are sufficient to lay open the heart of the matter, then one need go no further. Anything beyond this becomes labored. The gentleman rejects labored discourse, but the fool seizes upon it and makes it his treasure. Hence, the fool's words are hastily chosen and sketchy, contentious and wide of the mark, voluble and full of ferment. He is led astray by names, confused in his use of

---

[15]Reading *bian* instead of *chuan* in accordance with the suggestion of Ogyū Sorai.
[16]Reading *qu* instead of *tu*.
[17]No such lines are found in the present text of the *Odes*.

phrases, and there is no depth to his meaning. He struggles to advance but never reaches the heart of the matter; he expends great labor but achieves no result; he is greedy for reputation but wins none. The words of a wise man are easy to understand and easy to practice. Abide by them and you can easily make a place for yourself; carry them out and you will surely be able to obtain what you desire and avoid what you hate. The words of a fool are just the opposite. This is what the *Odes* means when it says:

> Were you a ghost or demon
> No one could see you.
> But you have a face and eyes
> Wherein men spy your dishonesty.
> So I have made this good song
> To expose to the full your evilness.[18]

   All those who maintain that desires must be gotten rid of before there can be orderly government fail to consider whether desires can be guided, but merely deplore the fact that they exist at all. All those who maintain that desires must be lessened before there can be orderly government fail to consider whether desires can be controlled, but merely deplore the fact that they are so numerous. Beings that possess desires and those that do not belong to two different categories—the categories of the living and the dead. But the possession or nonpossession of desires has nothing to do with good government or bad. Beings which have many desires and those which have few belong to two different categories. But this is a matter of the emotional nature of the being and has nothing to do with good government or bad.

---

[18]"Lesser Odes," *Herensi*, Mao text no. 199.

When one has a desire, he does not wait to make certain whether he can satisfy it, but immediately sets about trying to do so as best he can. The desire itself, which arises before one knows whether or not it can be satisfied, comes from the nature received at birth, while the search to satisfy it as best one can is directed by the mind. Thus a single desire which has sprung from the inborn nature may be directed and controlled in many different ways by the mind, until it becomes difficult to identify it with the original desire.[19] There is nothing a man desires more than life and nothing he hates more than death. And yet he may turn his back on life and choose death, not because he desires death and does not desire life, but because he cannot see his way clear to live, but only to die. Therefore, although a man's desires are excessive, his actions need not be so, because the mind will stop them short. If the dictates of the mind are in accord with just principles, then, although the desires are manifold, what harm will this be to good government? Conversely, even though there is a deficiency of desire, one's actions can still come up to the proper standard because the mind directs them. But if the dictates of the mind violate just principles, then, although the desires are few, the result will be far worse than merely bad government. Therefore, good or bad government depends upon the dictates of the mind, not upon the desires of the emotional nature. If you do not seek the cause of good or bad government where it exists, but only where it does not exist, though you may proclaim that you have found it, you will be wrong.

The basic nature of man is that which he receives from Heaven. The emotions are the substance of the nature and the desires are the responses of the emotions. It is impossible for the emotions not to believe that their desires can be satisfied and to refrain

---

[19]The meaning of this sentence is doubtful.

from seeking to satisfy them. But when they have decided that their desires can be satisfied, it must then be the function of the intellect to guide the search for satisfaction. Even a lowly gate-keeper cannot keep from having desires, for they are the insepa-rable attributes of the basic nature. On the other hand, even the Son of Heaven cannot completely satisfy all his desires. But al-though one cannot completely satisfy all his desires, he can come close to satisfying them, and although one cannot do away with all desires, he can control the search for satisfaction. (That is to say, one cannot completely satisfy all his desires, but by seeking to do so he can come close to satisfying them. Conversely, one cannot do away with all desires, and there will always be longings left un-satisfied; but the intellect can make an attempt to control the search for satisfaction.)[20] The Way in its positive aspect can lead one close to the satisfaction of all desires and in its negative aspect can serve to control the search for satisfaction. In this respect, there is nothing in the world to compare to it.

All men will abide by what they think is good and reject what they think is bad. It is inconceivable, therefore, that any man could understand that there is nothing in the world to compare to the Way, and yet not abide by it. Let us suppose, for exam-ple, that here is a man who desires to go south, regardless of the difficulties, and hates the thought of going north, no matter how easy it might be. Just because he may not be able to go as far south as he would like, is he likely to abandon the idea entirely and turn north instead? So men have certain things they desire, regardless of the difficulties involved, and certain things they hate, no matter how easily gotten. Simply because they cannot completely satisfy all their desires, is it likely that they will aban-

---

[20]The two sentences in parentheses simply repeat what has been said above, and are probably a gloss that has erroneously gotten into the text.

don the way which leads to the satisfaction of their desires and instead accept what they hate? Hence, if men approve the Way and abide by it, how is it possible to lead them astray and produce a state of disorder? And if they do not approve the Way and depart from it, how is it possible to improve them and produce a state of order? Therefore, the wise man discourses on the Way and nothing else, and the aims of petty men with their strange theories sink into obscurity.

When men acquire something, they never get only what they desire and nothing more; when men reject something, they never rid themselves only of what they hate and nothing more. Therefore, when men act, it must be on the basis of some scale and standard. If a balance is not properly adjusted, then heavy objects will go up in the air and men will suppose they are light, and light objects will sink down so that men suppose they are heavy. Hence men become deluded as to the true weight of the objects. Similarly, if men's standards are not correct, then misfortune may come in the guise of what they desire, and they will take it for good fortune, or good fortune may come in the guise of what they hate and they will mistake it for misfortune. In this way men become deluded as to the true nature of good and bad fortune. The Way is the proper standard for past and present. He who departs from the Way and makes arbitrary choices on the basis of his own judgment does not understand wherein fortune and misfortune lie.

If a man exchanges one object for another that is the same, then everyone will agree that he has neither gained nor lost anything. If he exchanges one object for two that are the same, then everyone will say that he has lost nothing but in fact has made a gain. But if he exchanges two objects for one, then everyone will agree that he has not gained but lost. Anyone who calculates can see that the gain lies with the greater number of objects and anyone who stops to think about it will choose the way that leads to the best results. No man will exchange two objects for one, because he knows well enough how to count. But to act in accordance with the Way is in fact like exchanging one object for two. How could it be a loss? To depart from the Way and make arbitrary choices on the basis of one's own judgment, however, is like exchanging two objects for one. How could it possibly be a gain? Any man who would actually exchange that which can gratify the desires of countless years for that which brings only a single moment of gratification[21] simply does not know how to do arithmetic.

But let us try delving deeper into the hidden aspects of the matter—those that are difficult to perceive. No man who derides true principles in his mind can fail to be led astray by undue attention to external objects. No one who pays undue attention to external objects can fail to feel anxiety in his mind. No man whose behavior departs from true principles can fail to be endangered by external forces. No man who is endangered by external forces can fail to feel terror in his mind. If the mind is full of anxiety and terror, then, though the mouth may be crammed with delicious food it will not recognize the flavor, though the ear listens to the music of bells and drums it will not recognize the sound, though the eye lights upon embroidered patterns it will not recognize their form, and though the body is clothed in warm, light garments and rests upon fine-woven mats, it will feel no ease. In such a case, a man may be confronted by all the loveliest things in the world and yet be unable to feel any gratification. Even if he should feel a moment's[22] gratification, he could never completely shake off his anxieties and fears. Hence, although he confronts all the loveliest things

---

[21]Reading *qie* instead of *xian*.
[22]Reading *jian* instead of *wen*.

in the world, he is overwhelmed with worry, and though he enjoys all the benefits in the world, he knows only loss.

What can a man like this hope for? Can he hope to gain possessions? Can he hope to nourish his health? Can he hope to prolong his life? He says he wants to satisfy his desires, and yet he sets out to do so by giving free license to his emotions. He says he wants to nourish his health, and yet he does things that endanger his body. He says he wants to increase his joy, and yet he afflicts his mind. He says he wants to win fame, and yet he allows his behavior to become reckless. Such a man might be enfeoffed as a lord and hailed as a ruler, but in fact he would be no different from an outlaw. He might ride in an elegant carriage and wear the cap of a high official, but he would still be no different from a needy peasant. This is what is called allowing the self to become the slave of things.

But if the mind is calm and at ease, then even beauties that are less than mediocre will gratify the eye, even sounds that are less than mediocre will gratify the ear. A meal of vegetables, a soup of boiled greens will gratify the mouth; robes of coarse cloth, shoes of coarse hemp will give ease to the body; a narrow room with rush blinds, a straw carpet, and a table and mat will give comfort to the form. Hence, one may not be able to enjoy all the most beautiful things in the world, and yet he can still increase his joy; he may not find a place among the famous and powerful, and yet he can still win fame. A man like this, if placed in the position of ruler, will do much for the world as a whole and give little thought to his private[23] pleasures. This is what it means to value the self and make other things work for you. Words that have a shallow basis, conduct that does not bear examining, schemes of ill repute—the gentleman is careful how he approaches these.

---

[23]Reading *si* instead of *he*.

⊰⊱ MAN'S NATURE IS EVIL

(Section 23)

Man's nature is evil; goodness is the result of conscious activity. The nature of man is such that he is born with a fondness for profit. If he indulges this fondness, it will lead him into wrangling and strife, and all sense of courtesy and humility will disappear. He is born with feelings of envy and hate, and if he indulges these, they will lead him into violence and crime, and all sense of loyalty and good faith will disappear. Man is born with the desires of the eyes and ears, with a fondness for beautiful sights and sounds. If he indulges these, they will lead him into license and wantonness, and all ritual principles and correct forms will be lost. Hence, any man who follows his nature and indulges his emotions will inevitably become involved in wrangling and strife, will violate the forms[1] and rules of society, and will end as a criminal. Therefore, man must first be transformed by the instructions of a teacher and guided by ritual principles, and only then will he be able to observe the dictates of courtesy and humility, obey the forms and rules of society, and achieve

---

[1]Reading *wen* instead of *fen*.

order. It is obvious from this, then, that man's nature is evil, and that his goodness is the result of conscious activity.

A warped piece of wood must wait until it has been laid against the straightening board, steamed, and forced into shape before it can become straight; a piece of blunt metal must wait until it has been whetted on a grindstone before it can become sharp. Similarly, since man's nature is evil, it must wait for the instructions of a teacher before it can become upright, and for the guidance of ritual principles before it can become orderly. If men have no teachers to instruct them, they will be inclined towards evil and not upright; and if they have no ritual principles to guide them, they will be perverse and violent and lack order. In ancient times the sage kings realized that man's nature is evil, and that therefore he inclines toward evil and violence and is not upright or orderly. Accordingly they created ritual principles and laid down certain regulations in order to reform man's emotional nature and make it upright, in order to train and transform it and guide it in the proper channels. In this way they caused all men to become orderly and to conform to the Way. Hence, today any man who takes to heart the instructions of his teacher, applies himself to his studies, and abides by ritual principles may become a gentleman, but anyone who gives free rein to his emotional nature, is content to indulge his passions, and disregards ritual principles becomes a petty man. It is obvious from this, therefore, that man's nature is evil, and that his goodness is the result of conscious activity.

Mencius states that man is capable of learning because his nature is good, but I say that this is wrong. It indicates that he has not really understood man's nature nor distinguished properly between the basic nature and conscious activity. The nature is that which is given by Heaven; you cannot learn it, you cannot acquire it by effort. Ritual principles, on the other hand, are created by sages; you can learn to apply them, you can work to bring them to completion. That part of man which cannot be learned or acquired by effort is called the nature; that part of him which can be acquired by learning and brought to completion by effort is called conscious activity. This is the difference between nature and conscious activity.

It is a part of man's nature that his eyes can see and his ears can hear. But the faculty of clear sight can never exist separately from the eye, nor can the faculty of keen hearing exist separately from the ear. It is obvious, then, that you cannot acquire clear sight and keen hearing by study. Mencius states that man's nature is good, and that all evil arises because he loses his original nature. Such a view, I believe, is erroneous. It is the way with man's nature that as soon as he is born he begins to depart from his original naïveté and simplicity, and therefore he must inevitably lose what Mencius regards as his original nature.[2] It is obvious from this, then, that the nature of man is evil.

Those who maintain that the nature is good praise and approve whatever has not departed from the original simplicity and naïveté of the child. That is, they consider that beauty belongs to the original simplicity and naïveté and goodness to the original mind in the same way that clear sight is inseparable from the eye and keen hearing from the ear. Hence, they maintain that [the nature possesses goodness] in the same way that the eye possesses clear vision or the ear keenness of hearing. Now it is the nature of man that when he is hungry he will desire satisfaction,

---

[2]Mencius, it will be recalled, stated: "The great man is he who does not lose his child's-heart" (*Mencius*, IVB, 12). If I understand Xunzi correctly, he is arguing that this "child's-heart," i.e., the simplicity and naïveté of the baby, will inevitably be lost by all men simply in the process of growing up, and therefore it cannot be regarded as the source of goodness.

when he is cold he will desire warmth, and when he is weary he will desire rest. This is his emotional nature. And yet a man, although he is hungry, will not dare to be the first to eat if he is in the presence of his elders, because he knows that he should yield to them, and although he is weary, he will not dare to demand rest because he knows that he should relieve others of the burden of labor. For a son to yield to his father or a younger brother to yield to his elder brother, for a son to relieve his father of work or a younger brother to relieve his elder brother—acts such as these are all contrary to man's nature and run counter to his emotions. And yet they represent the way of filial piety and the proper forms enjoined by ritual principles. Hence, if men follow their emotional nature, there will be no courtesy or humility; courtesy and humility in fact run counter to man's emotional nature. From this it is obvious, then, that man's nature is evil, and that his goodness is the result of conscious activity.

Someone may ask: if man's nature is evil, then where do ritual principles come from? I would reply: all ritual principles are produced by the conscious activity of the sages; essentially they are not products of man's nature. A potter molds clay and makes a vessel, but the vessel is the product of the conscious activity of the potter, not essentially a product of his human nature. A carpenter carves a piece of wood and makes a utensil, but the utensil is the product of the conscious activity of the carpenter, not essentially a product of his human nature. The sage gathers together his thoughts and ideas, experiments with various forms of conscious activity, and so produces ritual principles and sets forth laws and regulations. Hence, these ritual principles and laws are the products of the conscious activity of the sage, not essentially products of his human nature.

Phenomena such as the eye's fondness for beautiful forms, the ear's fondness for beautiful sounds, the mouth's fondness for delicious flavors, the mind's fondness for profit, or the body's fondness for pleasure and ease—these are all products of the emotional nature of man. They are instinctive and spontaneous; man does not have to do anything to produce them. But that which does not come into being instinctively but must wait for some activity to bring it into being is called the product of conscious activity. These are the products of the nature and of conscious activity respectively, and the proof that they are not the same. Therefore, the sage transforms his nature and initiates conscious activity; from this conscious activity he produces ritual principles, and when they have been produced he sets up rules and regulations. Hence, ritual principles and rules are produced by the sage. In respect to human nature the sage is the same as all other men and does not surpass[3] them; it is only in his conscious activity that he differs from and surpasses other men.

It is man's emotional nature to love profit and desire gain. Suppose now that a man has some wealth to be divided.[4] If he indulges his emotional nature, loving profit and desiring gain, then he will quarrel and wrangle even with his own brothers over the division. But if he has been transformed by the proper forms of ritual principle, then he will be capable of yielding even to a complete stranger. Hence, to indulge the emotional nature leads to the quarreling of brothers, but to be transformed by ritual principles makes a man capable of yielding to strangers.

Every man who desires to do good does so precisely because his nature is evil. A man whose accomplishments are meager longs for greatness; an ugly man longs for beauty; a man in cramped quarters longs for spaciousness; a poor man longs for wealth; a humble man longs for eminence. Whatever a man lacks

---

[3]Reading *guo* instead of *yi.*
[4]Omitting the words *dixiung*, which do not seem to belong here.

in himself he will seek outside. But if a man is already rich, he will not long for wealth, and if he is already eminent, he will not long for greater power. What a man already possesses in himself he will not bother to look for outside. From this we can see that men desire to do good precisely because their nature is evil. Ritual principles are certainly not a part of man's original nature. Therefore, he forces himself to study and to seek to possess them. An understanding of ritual principles is not a part of man's original nature, and therefore he ponders and plans and thereby seeks to understand them. Hence, man in the state in which he is born neither possesses nor understands ritual principles. If he does not possess ritual principles, his behavior will be chaotic, and if he does not understand them, he will be wild and irresponsible. In fact, therefore, man in the state in which he is born possesses this tendency towards chaos and irresponsibility. From this it is obvious, then, that man's nature is evil, and that his goodness is the result of conscious activity.

Mencius states that man's nature is good, but I say that this view is wrong. All men in the world, past and present, agree in defining goodness as that which is upright, reasonable, and orderly, and evil as that which is prejudiced, irresponsible, and chaotic. This is the distinction between good and evil. Now suppose that man's nature was in fact intrinsically upright, reasonable, and orderly—then what need would there be for sage kings and ritual principles? The existence of sage kings and ritual principles could certainly add nothing to the situation. But because man's nature is in fact evil, this is not so. Therefore, in ancient times the sages, realizing that man's nature is evil, that it is prejudiced and not upright, irresponsible and lacking in order, for this reason established the authority of the ruler to control it, elucidated ritual principles to transform it, set up laws and standards to correct it, and meted out strict punishments to restrain it. As a result, all the world achieved order and conformed to goodness. Such is the orderly government of the sage kings and the transforming power of ritual principles. Now let someone try doing away with the authority of the ruler, ignoring the transforming power of ritual principles, rejecting the order that comes from laws and standards, and dispensing with the restrictive power of punishments, and then watch and see how the people of the world treat each other. He will find that the powerful impose upon the weak and rob them, the many terrorize the few and extort from them, and in no time the whole world will be given up to chaos and mutual destruction. It is obvious from this, then, that man's nature is evil, and that his goodness is the result of conscious activity.

Those who are good at discussing antiquity must demonstrate the validity of what they say in terms of modern times; those who are good at discussing Heaven must show proofs from the human world. In discussions of all kinds, men value what is in accord with the facts and what can be proved to be valid. Hence if a man sits on his mat propounding some theory, he should be able to stand right up and put it into practice, and show that it can be extended over a wide area with equal validity. Now Mencius states that man's nature is good, but this is neither in accord with the facts, nor can it be proved to be valid. One may sit down and propound such a theory, but he cannot stand up and put it into practice, nor can he extend it over a wide area with any success at all. How, then, could it be anything but erroneous?

If the nature of man were good, we could dispense with sage kings and forget about ritual principles. But if it is evil, then we must go along with the sage kings and honor ritual principles. The straightening board is made because of the warped wood; the plumb line is employed because things are crooked; rulers are set up and ritual principles elucidated because the nature of man is evil. From this it is obvious, then, that man's nature is evil, and that his goodness is the result of conscious activity. A straight piece of wood does not have to wait for the straightening board to become straight; it is straight by nature. But a warped piece of wood must wait until it has been laid against the straightening board, steamed, and forced into shape before it can become straight, because by nature it is warped. Similarly, since man's nature is evil, he must wait for the ordering power of the sage kings and the transforming power of ritual principles; only then can he achieve order and conform to goodness. From this it is obvious, then, that man's nature is evil, and that his goodness is the result of conscious activity.

Someone may ask whether ritual principles and concerted conscious activity are not themselves a part of man's nature, so that for that reason the sage is capable of producing them. But I would answer that this is not so. A potter may mold clay and produce an earthen pot, but surely molding pots out of clay is not a part of the potter's human nature. A carpenter may carve wood and produce a utensil, but surely carving utensils out of wood is not a part of the carpenter's human nature. The sage stands in the same relation to ritual principles as the potter to the things he molds and produces. How, then, could ritual principles and concerted conscious activity be a part of man's basic human nature?

As far as human nature goes, the sages Yao and Shun possessed the same nature as the tyrant Jie or Robber Zhi, and the gentleman possesses the same nature as the petty man. Would you still maintain, then, that ritual principles and concerted conscious activity are a part of man's nature? If you do so, then what reason is there to pay any particular honor to Yao, Shun,[5] or the

---

[5]Reading *Shun* instead of *Yu* here and in the following sentence to conform to the sentence above.

gentleman? The reason people honor Yao, Shun, and the gentleman is that they are able to transform their nature, apply themselves to conscious activity, and produce ritual principles. The sage, then, must stand in the same relation to ritual principles as the potter to the things he molds and produces. Looking at it this way, how could ritual principles and concerted conscious activity be a part of man's nature? The reason people despise Jie, Robber Zhi, or the petty man is that they give free rein to their nature, follow their emotions, and are content to indulge their passions, so that their conduct is marked by greed and contentiousness. Therefore, it is clear that man's nature is evil, and that his goodness is the result of conscious activity.

Heaven did not bestow any particular favor upon Zengzi, Min Ziqian, or Xiaoyi that it withheld from other men.[6] And yet these three men among all others proved most capable of carrying out their duties as sons and winning fame for their filial piety. Why? Because of their thorough attention to ritual principles. Heaven has not bestowed any particular favor upon the inhabitants of Qi and Lu which it has withheld from the people of Qin. And yet when it comes to observing the duties of father and son and the separation of roles between husband and wife, the inhabitants of Qin cannot match the filial reverence and respect for proper form which marks the people of Qi and Lu.[7] Why? Because the people of Qin give free rein to their emotional nature, are content to indulge their passions, and are careless of ritual principles. It is certainly not due to any difference in human nature between the two groups.

---

[6]Min Ziqian and Zengzi were disciples of Confucius famed for their filial conduct. Xiaoyi is identified by commentators as the heir apparent of Gaozong—i.e., King Wuding—of the Yin dynasty.

[7]Reading *gong* instead of *ju*, *wen* instead of *fu*, and adding the words *Qinren* at the beginning of the sentence. Qi and Lu were of course the main centers of Confucian learning.

The man in the street can become a Yu.[8] What does this mean? What made the sage emperor Yu a Yu, I would reply, was the fact that he practiced benevolence and righteousness and abided by the proper rules and standards. If this is so, then benevolence, righteousness, and proper standards must be based upon principles which can be known and practiced. Any man in the street has the essential faculties needed to understand benevolence, righteousness, and proper standards, and the potential ability to put them into practice. Therefore it is clear that he can become a Yu.

Would you maintain that benevolence, righteousness, and proper standards are not based upon any principles that can be known and practiced? If so, then even a Yu could not have understood or practiced them. Or would you maintain that the man in the street does not have the essential faculties needed to understand them or the potential ability to put them into practice? If so, then you are saying that the man in the street in his family life cannot understand the duties required of a father or a son and in public life cannot comprehend the correct relationship between ruler and subject. But in fact this is not true. Any man in the street *can* understand the duties required of a father or a son and *can* comprehend the correct relationship between ruler and subject. Therefore, it is obvious that the essential faculties needed to understand such ethical principles and the potential ability to put them into practice must be a part of his make-up. Now if he takes these faculties and abilities and applies them to the principles of benevolence and righteousness, which we have already shown to be knowable and practicable,[9] then it

---

[8]This was apparently an old saying. Cf. *Mencius* VIB, 2: "Jia of Cao asked, 'It is said that all men may become Yaos or Shuns. Is this so?' Mencius replied, 'It is.'"
[9]Following the rearrangement of the text suggested by Tao Hongqing and Kanaya.

is obvious that he can become a Yu. If the man in the street applies himself to training and study, concentrates his mind and will, and considers and examines things carefully, continuing his efforts over a long period of time and accumulating good acts without stop, then he can achieve a godlike understanding and form a triad with Heaven and earth. The sage is a man who has arrived where he has through the accumulation of good acts.

You have said, someone may object, that the sage has arrived where he has through the accumulation of good acts. Why is it, then, that everyone is not able to accumulate good acts in the same way? I would reply: everyone is capable of doing so, but not everyone can be made to do so. The petty man is capable of becoming a gentleman, yet he is not willing to do so; the gentleman is capable of becoming a petty man but he is not willing to do so. The petty man and the gentleman are perfectly capable of changing places; the fact that they do not actually do so is what I mean when I say that they are capable of doing so but they cannot be made to do so. Hence, it is correct to say that the man in the street is *capable* of becoming a Yu but it is not necessarily correct to say that he will in fact find it possible to do so. But that he does not find it possible to do so does not prove that he is incapable of doing so.

A person with two feet is theoretically capable of walking to every corner of the earth, although in fact no one has ever found it possible to do so. Similarly, the artisan, the carpenter, the farmer, and the merchant are theoretically capable of exchanging professions, although in actual practice they find it impossible to do so. From this we can see that, although someone may be theoretically capable of becoming something, he may not in practice find it possible to do so. But although he does not find it possible to do so, this does not prove that he is not capable of doing so. To find it practically possible or impossible to do something and to be capable or incapable of doing something are two entirely different things. It is perfectly clear, then, that a man is theoretically capable of becoming something else.[10]

Yao asked Shun, "What are man's emotions like?" Shun replied, "Man's emotions are very unlovely things indeed! What need is there to ask any further? Once a man acquires a wife and children, he no longer treats his parents as a filial son should. Once he succeeds in satisfying his cravings and desires, he neglects his duty to his friends. Once he has won a high position and a good stipend, he ceases to serve his sovereign with a loyal heart. Man's emotions, man's emotions—they are very unlovely things indeed! What need is there to ask any further? Only the worthy man is different from this."[11]

There is the understanding of the sage, the understanding of the gentleman and man of breeding, the understanding of the petty man, and the understanding of the menial. He speaks many words but they are graceful and well ordered; all day he discourses on his reasons, employing a thousand different and varied modes of expression, and yet all that he says is united around a single principle: such is the understanding of the sage. He speaks little but what he says is brief and to the point, logical and clearly presented, as though laid out with a plumb line: such is the understanding of the gentleman and man of breeding. His words are all flattery, his actions irresponsible; whatever he does is shot through with error: such is the understanding of the petty man. His words are rapid and shrill but never to the point; his talents are varied and many but of no

---

[10]Adding *weichang* before the negative in accordance with the suggestion of Kubo Ai. But the sentence is far from clear.

[11]A similar passage is found in *Guanzi*, sec. 12, though without the anecdotal setting of a conversation between Yao and Shun.

practical use; he is full of subtle distinctions and elegant turns of phrase that serve no practical purpose; he ignores right or wrong, disdains to discuss crooked or straight, but seeks only to overpower the arguments of his opponent: such is the understanding of the menial.[12]

There is superior valor, there is the middle type of valor, and there is inferior valor. When proper standards prevail in the world, to dare to bring your own conduct into accord with them; when the Way of the former kings prevails, to dare to follow its dictates; to refuse to bow before the ruler of a disordered age, to refuse to follow the customs of the people of a disordered age; to accept poverty and hardship if they are in the cause of benevolent action; to reject wealth and eminence if they are not consonant with benevolent action; if the world recognizes you, to share[13] in the world's joys; if the world does not recognize you, to stand alone and without fear: this is superior valor. To be reverent in bearing and modest in intention; to value honor and make light of material goods; to dare to promote and honor the worthy, and reject and cast off the unworthy: such is the middle type of valor. To ignore your own safety in the quest for wealth; to make light of danger and try to talk your way out of every difficulty; to rely on lucky escapes; to ignore right and wrong, just and unjust, and seek only to overpower the arguments of your opponents: such is inferior valor.

Fanruo and Jushu were famous bows of ancient times, but if they had not first been subjected to presses and straighteners, they would never have become true of themselves. Cong of Duke Huan of Qi, Que of Taigong of Qi, Lu of King Wen of

---

[12]This last is of course aimed at the logicians.
[13]Reading *gong* instead of *ku*.

the Zhou, Hu of Lord Zhuang of Chu, and Ganjiang, Moye, Juque, and Bilü of King Helü of Wu were all famous swords of antiquity, but if they had not been subjected to the grindstone, they would never have become sharp, and if men of strength had not wielded them, they would never have been able to cut anything. Hualiu, Qiji, Xianli, and Luer were famous horses of antiquity, but if they had not been subjected to the restraint of bit and bridle and the threat of the whip, and driven by a master driver like Zaofu, they would never have succeeded in traveling a thousand *li* in one day.

In the same way a man, no matter how fine his nature or how keen his mind, must seek a worthy teacher to study under and good companions to associate with. If he studies under a worthy teacher, he will be able to hear about the ways of Yao, Shun, Yu, and Tang, and if he associates with good companions, he will be able to observe conduct that is loyal and respectful. Then, although he is not aware of it, he will day by day progress in the practice of benevolence and righteousness, for the environment he is subjected to will cause him to progress. But if a man associates with men who are not good, then he will hear only deceit and lies and will see only conduct that is marked by wantonness, evil, and greed. Then, although he is not aware of it, he himself will soon be in danger of severe punishment, for the environment he is subjected to will cause him to be in danger. An old text says, "If you do not know a man, look at his friends; if you do not know a ruler, look at his attendants." Environment is the important thing! Environment is the important thing!

Index

Other Works in the Columbia Asian Studies Series

TRANSLATIONS FROM THE ASIAN CLASSICS

Major Plays of Chikamatsu, tr. Donald Keene 1961

Four Major Plays of Chikamatsu, tr. Donald Keene. Paperback ed.
only. 1961; rev. ed. 1997

*Records of the Grand Historian of China, translated from the Shih chi of
Ssu-ma Ch'ien*, tr. Burton Watson, 2 vols. 1961

*Instructions for Practical Living and Other Neo-Confucian Writings by
Wang Yang-ming*, tr. Wing-tsit Chan 1963

Hsün Tzu: Basic Writings, tr. Burton Watson, paperback ed. only.
1963; rev. ed. 1996

Chuang Tzu: Basic Writings, tr. Burton Watson, paperback ed. only.
1964; rev. ed. 1996

The Mahābhārata, tr. Chakravarthi V. Narasimhan. Also in paperback ed. 1965; rev. ed. 1997

The Manyōshū, Nippon Gakujutsu Shinkōkai edition 1965

Su Tung-p'o: Selections from a Sung Dynasty Poet, tr. Burton Watson.
Also in paperback ed. 1965

Bhartrihari: Poems, tr. Barbara Stoler Miller. Also in paperback ed.
1967

Basic Writings of Mo Tzu, Hsün Tzu, and Han Fei Tzu, tr. Burton
Watson. Also in separate paperback eds. 1967

The Awakening of Faith, Attributed to Aśvaghosha, tr. Yoshito S. Hakeda. Also in paperback ed. 1967

Reflections on Things at Hand: The Neo-Confucian Anthology, comp. Chu Hsi and Lü Tsu-ch'ien, tr. Wing-tsit Chan 1967

The Platform Sutra of the Sixth Patriarch, tr. Philip B. Yampolsky. Also in paperback ed. 1967

Essays in Idleness: The Tsurezuregusa of Kenkō, tr. Donald Keene. Also in paperback ed. 1967

The Pillow Book of Sei Shōnagon, tr. Ivan Morris, 2 vols. 1967

Two Plays of Ancient India: The Little Clay Cart and the Minister's Seal, tr. J. A. B. van Buitenen 1968

The Complete Works of Chuang Tzu, tr. Burton Watson 1968

The Romance of the Western Chamber (Hsi Hsiang chi), tr. S. I. Hsiung. Also in paperback ed. 1968

The Manyōshū, Nippon Gakujutsu Shinkōkai edition. Paperback ed. only. 1969

Records of the Historian: Chapters from the Shih chi of Ssu-ma Ch'ien, tr. Burton Watson. Paperback ed. only. 1969

Cold Mountain: 100 Poems by the T'ang Poet Han-shan, tr. Burton Watson. Also in paperback ed. 1970

Twenty Plays of the Nō Theatre, ed. Donald Keene. Also in paperback ed. 1970

Chūshingura: The Treasury of Loyal Retainers, tr. Donald Keene. Also in paperback ed. 1971; rev. ed. 1997

The Zen Master Hakuin: Selected Writings, tr. Philip B. Yampolsky 1971

Chinese Rhyme-Prose: Poems in the Fu Form from the Han and Six Dynasties Periods, tr. Burton Watson. Also in paperback ed. 1971

Kūkai: Major Works, tr. Yoshito S. Hakeda. Also in paperback ed. 1972

The Old Man Who Does as He Pleases: Selections from the Poetry and Prose of Lu Yu, tr. Burton Watson 1973

The Lion's Roar of Queen Śrīmālā, tr. Alex and Hideko Wayman 1974

Courtier and Commoner in Ancient China: Selections from the History of the Former Han by Pan Ku, tr. Burton Watson. Also in paperback ed. 1974

Japanese Literature in Chinese, vol. 1: *Poetry and Prose in Chinese by Japanese Writers of the Early Period*, tr. Burton Watson 1975

Japanese Literature in Chinese, vol. 2: *Poetry and Prose in Chinese by Japanese Writers of the Later Period*, tr. Burton Watson 1976

Scripture of the Lotus Blossom of the Fine Dharma, tr. Leon Hurvitz. Also in paperback ed. 1976

Love Song of the Dark Lord: Jayadeva's Gītagovinda, tr. Barbara Stoler Miller. Also in paperback ed. Cloth ed. includes critical text of the Sanskrit. 1977; rev. ed. 1997

Ryōkan: Zen Monk-Poet of Japan, tr. Burton Watson 1977

Calming the Mind and Discerning the Real: From the Lam rim chen mo of Tsoṇ-kha-pa, tr. Alex Wayman 1978

The Hermit and the Love-Thief: Sanskrit Poems of Bhartrihari and Bilhaṇa, tr. Barbara Stoler Miller 1978

The Lute: Kao Ming's P'i-p'a chi, tr. Jean Mulligan. Also in paperback ed. 1980

A Chronicle of Gods and Sovereigns: Jinnō Shōtōki of Kitabatake Chikafusa, tr. H. Paul Varley 1980

Among the Flowers: The Hua-chien chi, tr. Lois Fusek 1982

Grass Hill: Poems and Prose by the Japanese Monk Gensei, tr. Burton Watson 1983

Doctors, Diviners, and Magicians of Ancient China: Biographies of Fang-shih, tr. Kenneth J. DeWoskin. Also in paperback ed. 1983

Theater of Memory: The Plays of Kālidāsa, ed. Barbara Stoler Miller. Also in paperback ed. 1984

The Columbia Book of Chinese Poetry: From Early Times to the Thirteenth Century, ed. and tr. Burton Watson. Also in paperback ed. 1984

Poems of Love and War: From the Eight Anthologies and the Ten Long Poems of Classical Tamil, tr. A. K. Ramanujan. Also in paperback ed. 1985

The Bhagavad Gita: Krishna's Counsel in Time of War, tr. Barbara Stoler Miller 1986

The Columbia Book of Later Chinese Poetry, ed. and tr. Jonathan Chaves. Also in paperback ed. 1986

The Tso Chuan: Selections from China's Oldest Narrative History, tr. Burton Watson 1989

Waiting for the Wind: Thirty-six Poets of Japan's Late Medieval Age, tr. Steven Carter 1989

Selected Writings of Nichiren, ed. Philip B. Yampolsky 1990

Saigyō, Poems of a Mountain Home, tr. Burton Watson 1990

The Book of Lieh Tzu: A Classic of the Tao, tr. A. C. Graham. Morningside ed. 1990

The Tale of an Anklet: An Epic of South India — The Cilappatikāram of Iḷaṅkō Aṭikaḷ, tr. R. Parthasarathy 1993

Waiting for the Dawn: A Plan for the Prince, tr. and introduction by Wm. Theodore de Bary 1993

Yoshitsune and the Thousand Cherry Trees: A Masterpiece of the Eighteenth-Century Japanese Puppet Theater, tr., annotated, and with introduction by Stanleigh H. Jones, Jr. 1993

The Lotus Sutra, tr. Burton Watson. Also in paperback ed. 1993

The Classic of Changes: A New Translation of the I Ching as Interpreted by Wang Bi, tr. Richard John Lynn 1994

Beyond Spring: Tz'u Poems of the Sung Dynasty, tr. Julie Landau 1994

The Columbia Anthology of Traditional Chinese Literature, ed. Victor H. Mair 1994

Scenes for Mandarins: The Elite Theater of the Ming, tr. Cyril Birch 1995

Letters of Nichiren, ed. Philip B. Yampolsky; tr. Burton Watson et al. 1996

Unforgotten Dreams: Poems by the Zen Monk Shōtetsu, tr. Steven D.
Carter 1997

The Vimalakirti Sutra, tr. Burton Watson 1997

Japanese and Chinese Poems to Sing: The Wakan rōei shū, tr. J.
Thomas Rimer and Jonathan Chaves 1997

A Tower for the Summer Heat, Li Yu, tr. Patrick Hanan 1998

Traditional Japanese Theater: An Anthology of Plays, Karen Brazell 1998

The Original Analects: Sayings of Confucius and His Successors
(0479–0249), E. Bruce Brooks and A. Taeko Brooks 1998

The Classic of the Way and Virtue: A New Translation of the Tao-te ching
of Laozi as Interpreted by Wang Bi, tr. Richard John Lynn 1999

The Four Hundred Songs of War and Wisdom: An Anthology of Poems
from Classical Tamil, The Puranāṇūṟu, eds. and trans. George L.
Hart and Hank Heifetz 1999

Original Tao: Inward Training (Nei-yeh) *and the Foundations of Taoist*
Mysticism, by Harold D. Roth 1999

Po Chü-i, Selected Poems, tr. Burton Watson 2000

Lao Tzu's Tao Te Ching: *A Translation of the Startling New Docu-*
ments Found at Guodian, Robert G. Henricks 2000

The Shorter Columbia Anthology of Traditional Chinese Literature, ed.
Victor H. Mair 2000

Mistress and Maid (Jiaohongji) by Meng Chengshun, tr. Cyril Birch
2001

Chikamatsu: Five Late Plays, tr. and ed. C. Andrew Gerstle

The Essential Lotus: Selections from the Lotus Sutra, tr. Burton Watson 2002

Early Modern Japanese Literature: An Anthology, 1600–1900, ed.
Haruo Shirane 2002

MODERN ASIAN LITERATURE

Modern Japanese Drama: An Anthology, ed. and tr. Ted. Takaya. Also
in paperback ed. 1979

Mask and Sword: Two Plays for the Contemporary Japanese Theater, by
Yamazaki Masakazu, tr. J. Thomas Rimer 1980

Yokomitsu Riichi, Modernist, Dennis Keene 1980

Nepali Visions, Nepali Dreams: The Poetry of Laxmiprasad Devkota, tr. David Rubin 1980

Literature of the Hundred Flowers, vol. 1: *Criticism and Polemics*, ed. Hualing Nieh 1981

Literature of the Hundred Flowers, vol. 2: *Poetry and Fiction*, ed. Hualing Nieh 1981

Modern Chinese Stories and Novellas, 1919 1949, ed. Joseph S. M. Lau, C. T. Hsia, and Leo Ou-fan Lee. Also in paperback ed. 1984

A View by the Sea, by Yasuoka Shōtarō, tr. Kären Wigen Lewis 1984

Other Worlds: Arishima Takeo and the Bounds of Modern Japanese Fiction, by Paul Anderer 1984

Selected Poems of Sō Chōngju, tr. with introduction by David R. McCann 1989

The Sting of Life: Four Contemporary Japanese Novelists, by Van C. Gessel 1989

Stories of Osaka Life, by Oda Sakunosuke, tr. Burton Watson 1990

The Bodhisattva, or Samantabhadra, by Ishikawa Jun, tr. with introduction by William Jefferson Tyler 1990

The Travels of Lao Ts'an, by Liu T'ieh-yün, tr. Harold Shadick. Morningside ed. 1990

Three Plays by Kōbō Abe, tr. with introduction by Donald Keene 1993

The Columbia Anthology of Modern Chinese Literature, ed. Joseph S. M. Lau and Howard Goldblatt 1995

Modern Japanese Tanka, ed. and tr. by Makoto Ueda 1996

Masaoka Shiki: Selected Poems, ed. and tr. by Burton Watson 1997

Writing Women in Modern China: An Anthology of Women's Literature from the Early Twentieth Century, ed. and tr. by Amy D. Dooling and Kristina M. Torgeson 1998

American Stories, by Nagai Kafū, tr. Mitsuko Iriye 2000

The Paper Door and Other Stories, by Shiga Naoya, tr. Lane Dunlop
2001

Grass for My Pillow, by Saiichi Maruya, tr. Dennis Keene 2002

STUDIES IN ASIAN CULTURE

*The Ōnin War: History of Its Origins and Background, with a Selective
Translation of the Chronicle of Ōnin*, by H. Paul Varley 1967

Chinese Government in Ming Times: Seven Studies, ed. Charles O.
Hucker 1969

The Actors' Analects (Yakusha Rongo), ed. and tr. by Charles J. Dunn
and Bungō Torigoe 1969

Self and Society in Ming Thought, by Wm. Theodore de Bary and the
Conference on Ming Thought. Also in paperback ed. 1970

A History of Islamic Philosophy, by Majid Fakhry, 2d ed. 1983

Phantasies of a Love Thief: The Caurapañcāśikā Attributed to Bilhaṇa,
by Barbara Stoler Miller 1971

Iqbal: Poet-Philosopher of Pakistan, ed. Hafeez Malik 1971

The Golden Tradition: An Anthology of Urdu Poetry, ed. and tr. Ahmed
Ali. Also in paperback ed. 1973

*Conquerors and Confucians: Aspects of Political Change in Late Yüan
China*, by John W. Dardess 1973

The Unfolding of Neo-Confucianism, by Wm. Theodore de Bary and
the Conference on Seventeenth-Century Chinese Thought. Also
in paperback ed. 1975

To Acquire Wisdom: The Way of Wang Yang-ming, by Julia Ching
1976

Gods, Priests, and Warriors: The Bhṛgus of the Mahābhārata, by Robert
P. Goldman 1977

Mei Yao-ch'en and the Development of Early Sung Poetry, by Jonathan
Chaves 1976

The Legend of Semimaru, Blind Musician of Japan, by Susan Matisoff
1977

Sir Sayyid Ahmad Khan and Muslim Modernization in India and Pakistan, by Hafeez Malik 1980

The Khilafat Movement: Religious Symbolism and Political Mobilization in India, by Gail Minault 1982

The World of K'ung Shang-jen: A Man of Letters in Early Ch'ing China, by Richard Strassberg 1983

The Lotus Boat: The Origins of Chinese Tz'u Poetry in T'ang Popular Culture, by Marsha L. Wagner 1984

Expressions of Self in Chinese Literature, ed. Robert E. Hegel and Richard C. Hessney 1985

Songs for the Bride: Women's Voices and Wedding Rites of Rural India, by W. G. Archer; eds. Barbara Stoler Miller and Mildred Archer 1986

The Confucian Kingship in Korea: Yŏngjo and the Politics of Sagacity, by JaHyun Kim Haboush 1988

COMPANIONS TO ASIAN STUDIES

Approaches to the Oriental Classics, ed. Wm. Theodore de Bary 1959

Early Chinese Literature, by Burton Watson. Also in paperback ed. 1962

Approaches to Asian Civilizations, eds. Wm. Theodore de Bary and Ainslie T. Embree 1964

The Classic Chinese Novel: A Critical Introduction, by C. T. Hsia. Also in paperback ed. 1968

Chinese Lyricism: Shih Poetry from the Second to the Twelfth Century, tr. Burton Watson. Also in paperback ed. 1971

A Syllabus of Indian Civilization, by Leonard A. Gordon and Barbara Stoler Miller 1971

Twentieth-Century Chinese Stories, ed. C. T. Hsia and Joseph S. M. Lau. Also in paperback ed. 1971

A Syllabus of Chinese Civilization, by J. Mason Gentzler, 2d ed. 1972

A Syllabus of Japanese Civilization, by H. Paul Varley, 2d ed. 1972

An Introduction to Chinese Civilization, ed. John Meskill, with the assistance of J. Mason Gentzler 1973

An Introduction to Japanese Civilization, ed. Arthur E. Tiedemann 1974

Ukifune: Love in the Tale of Genji, ed. Andrew Pekarik 1982

The Pleasures of Japanese Literature, by Donald Keene 1988

A Guide to Oriental Classics, eds. Wm. Theodore de Bary and Ainslie T. Embree; 3d edition ed. Amy Vladeck Heinrich, 2 vols. 1989

INTRODUCTION TO ASIAN CIVILIZATIONS

Wm. Theodore de Bary, General Editor

Sources of Japanese Tradition, 1958; paperback ed., 2 vols., 1964. 2d ed., vol. 1, 2001, compiled by Wm. Theodore de Bary, Donald Keene, George Tanabe, and Paul Varley

Sources of Indian Tradition, 1958; paperback ed., 2 vols., 1964. 2d ed., 2 vols., 1988

Sources of Chinese Tradition, 1960, paperback ed., 2 vols., 1964. 2d ed., vol. 1, 1999, compiled by Wm. Theodore de Bary and Irene Bloom; vol. 2, 2000, compiled by Wm. Theodore de Bary and Richard Lufrano

Sources of Korean Tradition, 1997; 2 vols., vol. 1, 1997, compiled by Peter H. Lee and Wm. Theodore de Bary; vol. 2, 2001, compiled by Yŏngho Ch'oe, Peter H. Lee, and Wm. Theodore de Bary

NEO-CONFUCIAN STUDIES

Instructions for Practical Living and Other Neo-Confucian Writings by Wang Yang-ming, tr. Wing-tsit Chan 1963

Reflections on Things at Hand: The Neo-Confucian Anthology, comp. Chu Hsi and Lü Tsu-ch'ien, tr. Wing-tsit Chan 1967

Self and Society in Ming Thought, by Wm. Theodore de Bary and the Conference on Ming Thought. Also in paperback ed. 1970

The Unfolding of Neo-Confucianism, by Wm. Theodore de Bary and the Conference on Seventeenth-Century Chinese Thought. Also in paperback ed. 1975

Principle and Practicality: Essays in Neo-Confucianism and Practical Learning, eds. Wm. Theodore de Bary and Irene Bloom. Also in paperback ed. 1979

The Syncretic Religion of Lin Chao-en, by Judith A. Berling 1980

The Renewal of Buddhism in China: Chu-hung and the Late Ming Synthesis, by Chün-fang Yü 1981

Neo-Confucian Orthodoxy and the Learning of the Mind-and-Heart, by Wm. Theodore de Bary 1981

Yüan Thought: Chinese Thought and Religion Under the Mongols, eds. Hok-lam Chan and Wm. Theodore de Bary 1982

The Liberal Tradition in China, by Wm. Theodore de Bary 1983

The Development and Decline of Chinese Cosmology, by John B. Henderson 1984

The Rise of Neo-Confucianism in Korea, by Wm. Theodore de Bary and JaHyun Kim Haboush 1985

Chiao Hung and the Restructuring of Neo-Confucianism in Late Ming, by Edward T. Ch'ien 1985

Neo-Confucian Terms Explained: Pei-hsi tzu-i, by Ch'en Ch'un, ed. and trans. Wing-tsit Chan 1986

Knowledge Painfully Acquired: K'un-chih chi, by Lo Ch'in-shun, ed. and trans. Irene Bloom 1987

To Become a Sage: The Ten Diagrams on Sage Learning, by Yi T'oegye, ed. and trans. Michael C. Kalton 1988

The Message of the Mind in Neo-Confucian Thought, by Wm. Theodore de Bary 1989